Contemporary Discourse
in the Field of
PHYSICS™

Changes Within Physical Systems and/or Conservation of Energy and Momentum

An Anthology of Current Thought

Edited by Ray Villard

The Rosen Publishing Group, Inc., New York

Published in 2006 by The Rosen Publishing Group, Inc.
29 East 21st Street, New York, NY 10010

Library of Congress Cataloging-in-Publication Data

Changes within physical systems and/or conservation of energy
and momentum : an anthology of current thought/edited by Ray
Villard.—1st ed.
    p. cm.—(Contemporary discourse in the field of physics)
Includes bibliographical references and index.
ISBN 1-4042-0404-0 (lib. bdg.)
1. Astrophysics. 2. Cosmology. 3. Celestial mechanics. I. Villard,
Ray. II. Series.
QB461.C48 2006
523.01—dc22

                                                              2004025840

Manufactured in the United States of America

On the cover (clockwise from top right): Patterns of light on
a white surface; swinging clock pendulum; portrait of Sir Isaac
Newton; liquid crystal.

MAR   2007

CONTENTS

Introduction

Contrary to the universe being static, or non-moving, which it was once believed to be, the cosmos is a place where energy and momentum are continuously exchanged. But despite this rapid change of matter into energy and energy into matter, matter and energy are neither created nor destroyed. The universe is a zero-sum system. Matter and energy are neither added nor taken away. They can only be exchanged with each other.

This anthology presents a sample of articles that discuss how matter and energy interact in nature, under extreme conditions, to construct the universe around us. We'll see again and again that even the most extreme and bizarre phenomena in nature always obey the fundamental laws of the conservation of energy and momentum. Through an ongoing exchange of potential (stored) and kinetic (released) energy ever since the beginning of the universe, stars, galaxies, and planets have formed. The early universe was a vast reserve of potential energy locked up in matter. This potential energy, in the form of gravity, allowed for the formation of massive accumulations of stars, or galaxies. In the same way but on a smaller scale, gravity has allowed for the creation of planets and entire solar systems.

Several articles in this anthology explore the emerging realization that dense and compact objects like black holes are tremendous reserves of gravitational energy. Black holes are the most extreme example of intense gravitational fields. A black hole's gravity is so strong that mass can be converted to energy with great efficiency within it. This energy can manifest as light and can power some of the most brilliant phenomena in the universe.

One article here, titled "The Missing Black Hole Link," explores how super-massive black holes can actually form when two smaller black holes collide. It appears that black holes can also grow through dynamical phenomena called mass segregation, in which massive objects like black holes transfer momentum to smaller objects in a star cluster. These black holes lose momentum and move to the centers of clusters of stars. Once there, the black holes merge to make even more massive black holes, which then collectively move to the hub of a galaxy.

It was once thought that black holes should exist forever as compact reservoirs of gravitational energy. However, it is now predicted that they transfer some of their energy back into space. This effect, called "evaporation," is when particles of matter are produced at the periphery of the black hole (the event horizon, which marks the boundary from which matter cannot escape).

These particles escape into space and sap some of the black hole's energy until the hole becomes so weak that it abruptly loses all of its gravitational energy into space in a burst of radiation.

The article "Hawking Slays His Own Paradox, but Colleagues Are Wary" suggests that we may see evidence of this happening in the universe around us now. The esteemed British physicist and black hole theorist Steven Hawking has even proposed that evaporating black holes can even release information about what previously fell into them. Prior to this theory, physicists worried that the idea of a black hole permanently swallowing matter and energy violated the law of the conservation of matter and energy.

The gravitational transfer of energy between moving bodies is also explored in several articles here. This transfer has driven the formation of stars, planets, and moons. Another article, titled "The Missing Moon of Sedna," studies the farthest large object known in the solar system today, the planetoid Sedna, which shows evidence of being gravitationally perturbed by a bypassing star. One possibility of this perturbation is that Sedna robbed some of the star's momentum and, as a result, was kicked into a larger orbit around the Sun.

Along these lines of the conservation of energy and momentum in the solar system, there is increasing evidence that the young solar system has been involved in many dynamic interactions in which the momentum and kinetic energy of celestial bodies have been exchanged. The article "It's Not Easy to Make the

Moon" explores how our own Moon may have been formed from a collision between Earth and another large object in the young solar system. A complex, seesawing series of energy transfers between Earth-orbiting debris converted the scattered objects into our Moon.

The early solar system was cluttered with rocky bodies called planetesimals. It was like a billiards table cluttered with billiard balls. The exchange of momentum among these bodies caused mergers between the bodies, as described in "It's Not Easy to Make the Moon," or flung debris out of the solar system. Today most of the former objects are part of planets or moons, but not totally. The residual rocky debris accounts for only half the mass of our Moon (which itself is merely one-eightieth the mass of Earth). The rest is believed to be scattered between the orbits of Mars and Jupiter in the asteroid belt.

Space probes sent to asteroids continue studying their physical makeup and can even be used to pre-cisely estimate an asteroid's mass by measuring its gravitational pull on the spacecraft. Some asteroids have had their orbits changed through gravitational interactions with other objects. These orbits sometimes crisscross Earth's orbit. Some of the asteroids following these paths will eventually collide with Earth. Though an asteroid's mass is a tiny fraction of Earth's mass, its rapid speed around the Sun makes it a lethal "inter-planetary bullet." An asteroid just a few kilometers across, about the size of a small town, would unleash a devastating amount of kinetic energy if it hit Earth. In the article "Deflecting NEOs in Route of Collision with

8

the Earth" explores how we can use the laws of conservation of energy and momentum to divert asteroids that are on course to collide with Earth, thereby saving our civilization.

Other articles in this anthology explore the technological application of what we have learned about the dynamic universe. Several explore the possibility of building machines that can effectively be powered by converting mass into energy in novel ways. At one end of the spectrum are nanomachines, the smallest conceivable physical man-made objects that someday might perform a variety of practical work for us. Such machines could easily fit inside a single blood cell and perform medical tasks inside the human body. What we would consider very small amounts of energy may be able to be manipulated among atoms to power these devices.

At the other extreme is the quest for rocket engines that can yield enough energy to propel a probe extremely long distances, such as to stars that possess planets, which we might be able to explore for life. Such a starship requires looking to nature for ideas on how to generate energy as efficiently as possible in order to allow us to travel these great distances.

The science experiments and observations described in this anthology are a snapshot of how physicists are at last mastering a deep understating of the interchanging roles between matter and energy and momentum in our dynamic universe. Today's physics at last brings together the worlds of the nearly infinitely–large and the infinitesimally small. The universe at large sweeps us back into time to explore how the balance between matter and energy and momentum has been so chaotic, yet precise enough to create stars, planets, and people. —RV

Energy, Momentum, and Interstellar Travel

1

Rockets are a wonderful example of the principle of conservation of energy and momentum. As a rocket's fuel, or energy, is forced in one direction, the rocket's momentum is transferred in the opposite direction.

This type of conservation of energy and momentum is described in Isaac Newton's third law of motion, which states that for every action, there is an equal and opposite reaction. Newton's third law poses a problem, however, for spaceships traveling extremely long distances, such as to Alpha Centauri, our nearest star, which is 4.3 light-years away. These rockets need to carry a lot of fuel to get them to travel these extremely long distances. This large quantity of fuel adds mass to the rocket. The more fuel the rocket carries, the more energy is required to propel the additional mass. Eventually, any added fuel is used almost exclusively to propel the added mass the fuel creates. This puts serious limitations on just how far into the universe we can travel. As a result, engineers are trying to design rockets that *generate the most energy from the least amount of fuel in order to provide them with the momentum to travel these long distances.*

The following article examines some alternative energy sources such as antimatter annihilation, lasers, and giant tethers, which scientists are experimenting with in order to achieve this goal. Each of these methods is a modern-day example of how humans are attempting to overcome the obstacles posed by the conservation of energy and momentum in order to break new scientific ground. —RV

From "Prospects for an Interstellar Mission: Hard Technology Limits but Surprising Physics Possibilities"
by Bernard Haisch and Alfonso Rueda
Mercury, July/August 2000

How can we reach another star in a timely fashion? Extrapolating our best current technology into the future is like trying to somehow soup-up Magellan's sailing ship to circumnavigate the globe in ninety minutes.

· The concept of interstellar missions of exploration, discovery, and, let's be honest, sheer adventure, took hold of our cultural imagination with the advent of the *Star Trek* television series in 1966. Dressed up in clever, quasi-scientific language like "warp drive" and "impulse engine," the idea had a certain air of plausibility for the public.

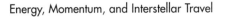
Indeed, the notion of interstellar travel has probably come to seem inevitable to the public at large. Once upon a time it would have seemed like a miracle to cross the ocean . . . but Columbus did that by and by (even though long after the Vikings!). So why not assume we will one day sail the ocean of space?

Unfortunately, the problems are more fundamental. They have more to do with basic physics than with "mere" technology. But a sea change has occurred nonetheless. Although there are no known or plausible technologies that would make interstellar travel possible, the concept of an interstellar mission has become a legitimate topic for scientific discussion in NASA circles.

Pushing Tin (and Fuel)

Looking for a better rocket to get us to the stars would be like trying to upgrade Columbus's Nina, Pinta, and Santa Maria with wings to speed up the Atlantic crossing time. A jet airliner is not a better sailing ship. It is a different thing entirely.

A typical car weighing perhaps 3,000 pounds carries about 100 pounds of gasoline in its fuel tank. The fuel is a small percentage of the total mass, in this case under four percent. The ratio of fuel to vehicle is much less than one (1/30), and that works fine because you can stop and "fill 'er up" anytime. For a 747 jumbo jet leaving San Francisco for London, the ratio of fuel to dry weight of the airplane is much higher: the jet fuel may amount to as much as 1/3 of the mass of the unfueled aircraft because you want to make the trip without refueling. This ratio of fuel to vehicle gets larger and larger for a rocket. The propellant weighs more than the rocket itself, making the ratio greater than one. And that is the beginning of a major problem.

Once the ratio gets to be greater than one, you quickly enter a no-win situation. If you wanted to put the Space Shuttle into a higher orbit, you could—in principle anyway—use more propellant, but you have to then launch more propellant and a bigger rocket to carry the additional propellant. Pretty soon you are using your additional propellant almost exclusively to launch more propellant. Your gain in either more payload or longer range gets less and less the higher the ratio of propellant to rocket. And it just keeps getting worse.

The other killer is that it takes as much propellant to slow down as to speed up. Slowing down is just speeding up in reverse. Now, there may be mitigating circumstances. The Moon trips were possible because the Moon's gravity is much less than Earth's, so it took much less energy (per unit mass) to fight the Moon's lower gravity and achieve a soft landing than it took to launch off Earth. You gain twice this way because leaving the Moon is also easy in the same proportion. Then, finally, the astronauts used Earth's atmosphere to achieve braking. All of these mitigating circumstances enabled the Moon landing and return adventure to succeed, but we still had to launch a mighty, multi-stage Saturn rocket as tall as a 35-story building . . . just to get back one little capsule and three guys splashing down in the ocean.

How much conventional propellant would you need to launch the Space Shuttle to a speed that would carry it in 100 years to Alpha Centauri, the nearest star system and a mere 4.3 lightyears away? The answer is that a rocket the size of Earth filled with chemical fuel would be insufficient. Even a rocket the size of the Sun would not do. And that is for only a flyby. If you want to slow down, land on a planet—which one hopes is there to land on—and then launch back home again finally to land safely on Earth, you are totally out of luck. A rocket the size of the entire visible Universe would be too small. The problem of adding more and more propellant just to propel the propellant skyrockets to infinity. A better chemical rocket is simply not an interstellar option.

This exemplifies the propulsion-mass problem. Indeed, even within the Solar System, if you want to visit and return from other planets, the problem with rockets looms large. However, here it is at least possible to consider refueling by somehow processing material to be found at or near the destination. Carrying your propulsion fuel with you, like a turtle and his shell, becomes a show stopper, though, for interstellar exploration.

But moving beyond chemical propulsion, what if such an efficient propellant could be found that, like a car with its gas tank, the ratio of fuel to rocket mass were again well below one? It is the fact that the propellant to rocket ratio is over one that sends the problem soaring out of control. Where can we look to find the real world analogs of Captain Kirk's manageable-sized dilithium crystals (which must be pretty compact since there always seems to be plenty of room left over for Commander Scotty to be tinkering and frantically running around in his engine room)?

Propellant Matters

A survey of ideas took place in July 1998. The Advanced Concepts Office at the Jet Propulsion Laboratory and the Office of Space Science at NASA headquarters jointly sponsored a workshop at Caltech entitled "Robotic Interstellar Exploration in the Next Century." Essentially all known, credible, interstellar propulsion ideas were discussed.

In broad terms there are four possible types of on-board engines: chemical, fission, fusion, and antimatter. Rocket-type propulsion works in the vacuum of space because you do not need to push or pull on any medium the way a propeller does in air or water. You carry along your own matter (this becomes the problem of course) which you expel out the back of the rocket to push it forward. The vacuum not withstanding, you could push yourself forward by throwing bricks out the rear; naturally this is not very efficient.

There are two properties that characterize a propellant: for each kilogram of the stuff, how much force do you generate when it is expelled? This is measured by a quantity called specific impulse which tells you how much acceleration you can get over how long a period of time from a given propellant. And the second important fuel property: how much energy can you extract from each kilogram of propellant? Call this the energy content.

You need both a high specific impulse and a high energy content to have an efficient rocket. They do not necessarily go together: a fuel with a relatively low

16

energy content may give a relatively high specific impulse and vice versa. It is instructive, though, to take the absolutely best possible case and see where that leaves the possibility of interstellar travel when you have to carry your fuel along as in a rocket.

No matter what your specific impulse, you cannot do better than to convert all of your available propellant energy into the kinetic energy of the rocket. That is, of course, wildly optimistic, but it simplifies things by letting us concentrate solely on energy. A benchmark for discussion at the NASA/Caltech meeting was a forty-year mission. To get to Alpha Centauri in this time would require a speed of about one-tenth the speed of light (0.1 c), since Alpha Centauri is just over four lightyears distant. At that modest speed you can still calculate the kinetic energy of your starship using ordinary Newtonian physics. It is simply mv^2, where m is the mass and v the speed of the starship.

There is no more energy-efficient fuel than anti-matter. Letting matter and antimatter combine gives you up to 100 percent energy efficiency . . . When you equate the rocket kinetic energy and the mass energy of the anti-matter, you find that an amount of matter-antimatter fuel that is only 0.5 percent of the mass of the starship is all you would need to get to 0.1 c. Of course, if you want to slow down at the end of your forty-year mission, you would need just as much again. So the bottom line appears to be that a starship with one percent matter-antimatter fuel could reach a speed of 0.1 c, get to Alpha Centauri in forty years, and brake at some planet—that one hopes is there—in that star system.

At first glance this seems remarkably encouraging. Unfortunately ugly details quickly loom large. First of all, just because the matter-energy conversion is 100 percent efficient does not mean that you can give that energy with 100 percent efficiency to the starship. This goes back to specific impulse considerations. There is at least a factor of ten loss in efficiency, so raise the matter-antimatter fuel to rocket percentage from one percent to ten percent. Being about the same ratio as that of full gas tank to car, ten percent still looks acceptable, but next you have to consider how much antimatter this really amounts to and its implications.

Since the plan is to be as optimistic as possible to find out where there is a true hard limit, a show-stopper no matter what, let us also assume that we will know how to put the crew into suspended animation so that we can use a starship the size of the Space Shuttle rather than the size of an aircraft carrier (and who would even want to live on the latter for four decades?). Assume a 100-ton vehicle, and we now have a requirement of ten tons of matter-antimatter fuel, or five tons of pure antimatter as a requirement. Double that to ten tons of antimatter for a round-trip.

There are no free sources of antimatter. Since it annihilates on contact with matter, there is clearly no supply around to tap; you cannot just go mine for it like uranium. But antimatter can be manufactured in particle accelerators and there are techniques to store small amounts of it. With some upgrading to tailor the facility to do this, the United States's Brookhaven National Laboratory could turn out one-tenth of a billionth of a

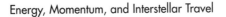

gram of antiprotons per year. Similar capabilities exist at the Center for European Nuclear Research (CERN) near Geneva and the Institute for High Energy Physics in Russia. But the required ten tons of antiprotons would be equivalent to about ten million grams. The difference between what we can manufacture in a year of production and what we would need for a single roundtrip becomes an enormous factor of 10^{17} (i.e., a hundred million billion). This is more than a big gap.

Even if we could easily manufacture the required quantity of antimatter, however, we would have a tremendous problem on our hands. The huge amount of energy contained in five tons of antimatter—which is great for propulsion—is, of course, a disastrous storage problem here on Earth. It would be equivalent to about 200,000 Megatons of TNT, which is ten million Hiroshima-energy bombs. For comparison, the largest (then) Soviet hydrogen bomb tests in the 1960s involved explosions of a mere 100 Megatons or so.

In terms of designing a starship for a single, one-way trip based on rocket-style, onboard propulsion, this is as good as it gets! Rocket-style, carry-your-fuel propulsion is the wrong approach for a starship.

Leave the Fuel Behind

An alternative to carrying your engine and fuel along is to leave both behind. This way you do not get into the exponentially losing situation of having to accelerate your propellant. A tiny fraction of the same energy supply will get the same job done if all you have to accelerate is the vehicle itself. The problem now, of course, is to transmit the propulsion from the source to the vehicle. Two such schemes have been proposed and were discussed at the NASA/Caltech workshop: lasers and particle beams.

When you are sitting next to a window with sunlight shining on you, you feel the energy of the light in the form of heat, but you do not notice any force or pressure from the light. But light does carry both energy and momentum. When sunlight lands on a small particle in space and is absorbed, the momentum of the light is transferred to the particle and that creates a measurable force on the particle. This is the very process that forms a comet's tail. As the snowy iceball that is the comet's nucleus approaches the Sun and begins to evaporate, radiation pressure from the sunlight pushes the evaporating gas and dust outward, creating the tail that is millions of miles long.

A powerful laser can exert a great deal of force, and that is the basis of the laser sail concept. Instead of carrying vast amounts of propellant to power an onboard engine, a laser-beam starship would literally sail off into space with no need for an engine at all. It would ride on the force provided by a beam of light from a giant laser that never has to leave the Solar System. A perfectly reflecting sail is even more efficient—by a factor of two—than one that absorbs the light, and this could be made out of very flimsy material, something like super high-tech aluminum foil, if constructed in Earth's orbit.

A major problem with this concept for interstellar considerations is size. A laser can focus a beam of light to its maximum theoretical concentration. If we assume that a sail could be assembled and held in place that was as large as 10 km in diameter, we would want the laser to still concentrate virtually all of its light on the sail even when that sail is halfway to the nearest star, otherwise we lose more and more of the force. If the light beam spreads to only ten times the size of the sail, the loss of force is 99 percent since it is area that matters. Yet to keep this high degree of focus, the laws of optics dictate that the laser must effectively be a lens or mirror 1,000 km in diameter to achieve this for visible light . . . You can trade off the sail diameter against the laser lens diameter. Make the sail ten times bigger and you can use a laser with a ten-times smaller lens. You then have a 100-km sail and 100-km laser lens. So we see that all possible combinations stretch credibility.

Apart from the problem of requiring vast sails or gigantic lasers, there is a good reason to get worried even if you could manage to concentrate all the laser power on the sail even at the halfway point to Alpha Centauri. And that is, what do you do for the next half of the trip to slow down? It is a one-way push. You can jettison your sail and coast, but you cannot stop.

Even if that were not problem enough, there is a time-delay feedback problem that gets worse and worse. Taking the laser-driven sail as an example, let us assume that a mission propelled by a 10-km diameter light sail is halfway (2×10^{13} km) to Alpha Centauri when a beam problem reaches the vehicle. A misalignment of the laser of no more than one part in a trillion, which occurred back on Earth two years ago, is now reaching the vehicle causing the beam to miss the light sail. Owing to the speed-of-light limitation, it will be another two years before any news of this problem transmitted by the spacecraft can reach Earth. It will be yet another two years before the correction from Earth will reach the spacecraft. But by then the vehicle may have drifted out of its trajectory sufficiently, owing to the effects of interaction with the interstellar medium (or other causes), that it is still out of the beam. Indeed, any drift of the vehicle from a line-of-sight trajectory will cause the same uncorrectable problem in the first place since there is no way to know where the vehicle is "now" (in the sense of where the beam is supposed to hit). This illustrates the inherent problem of speed-of-light caused time delay in any feedback loop. It would be all too easy—in fact, probably unavoidable—to have a mission using this propulsion mechanism "lost in space without a paddle" due to the slightest error . . .

One other scheme that is clever in principle was presented at the NASA/Caltech meeting: the use of giant tethers. Such a tether is simply a very long wire dangling in space. When a conducting wire is moved perpendicular to a magnetic field, a current is induced in the wire, which can be used as a source of electrical power. This has been the motivation for several space experiments in recent years. But a rather different application can be envisioned using the interstellar magnetic field to generate a propulsive force.

Instead of using the interstellar magnetic field to originate a current, you use an onboard source of power to create your own current in a long tether. There is a law in electrodynamics that tells you that if you have a current flowing in a wire perpendicular to a magnetic field, there will be a (Lorentz) force perpendicular to both. A current plus the interstellar magnetic field gives you a potentially propulsive force . . .

The electromagnetic zero-point field, or more generally, the quantum vacuum, offers four possibilities that *may* someday yield the technology to travel to other stars: extraction of energy, generation of forces, and, most intriguingly, perhaps even manipulation of inertia and gravitation. At present these are highly speculative possibilities, but the exploration of these ideas seems at least as worthwhile as trying to work around the formidable obstacles and insuperable limitations we've already discussed here.

Reprinted by permission of *Mercury* magazine and the Astronomical Society of the Pacific. www.astrosociety.org

Centrifugal means "center fleeing." Centrifugal force, therefore, is a force that flees the center of the axis of motion of a turning body. You experience centrifugal force when driving around a curve in a car. Centrifugal force pushes you away from the axis of rotation.

Centrifugal force is an example of the conservation of energy and momentum. When an object at the end of a rotating tether, such as a rock tied to a string, is let go, angular momentum is conserved. This is why the rock flies away

once it breaks free of the string. The amount of energy transferred is directly proportional to the rock's speed of rotation.

Following this model, scientists are now using the principle of the conservation of energy and momentum in the form of a space tether in order to propel spacecraft far from Earth. A space tether would connect two satellites that are in Earth's orbit. One satellite would orbit closer to Earth. Since gravity decreases with distance, the difference between the two satellites' distances would affect how strongly Earth's gravitational pull influenced them. The closer satellite would feel a stronger gravitational pull than the farther satellite. Thus, the gravitational difference between the two satellites would keep the tether between them taut.

When the less massive satellite is released from the tether, it would use the momentum gained from Earth's rotation to fly to its destination. This concept has not yet been attempted, but it is a simple strategy based on the conservation of energy and momentum for propelling spacecraft far beyond Earth. —RV

From "A Little Physics and a Lot of String"
by Patrick Barry
NASA.gov, July 9, 2000

It's amazing what you can do with a little physics and a lot of string.

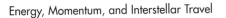

You could generate electrical power for orbiting satellites. Or you could prevent the International Space Station's orbit from deteriorating. You could also force an object in orbit around the Earth to fall into the atmosphere and burn up.

These are just some of the applications being explored by NASA scientists and private companies for a remarkably elegant technology called space tethers.

"A space tether is a long string or a wire that connects two objects that are in orbit together," said Dr. Dennis Gallagher, a research scientist at NASA's Marshall Space Flight Center. "An orbiting tether tends to straighten out along a radial line because the force of gravity varies slightly along its length. The pull of gravity is stronger nearest the Earth and weakest furthest away. That means there is a net force on a tether which stretches it and keeps the line taut. This isn't just an exercise in physics, though, these tethers have lots of useful applications." . . .

"There are two types of tethers: electromagnetic tethers and momentum-exchange tethers," says Dr. Robert Hoyt, president of Tethers Unlimited, Inc., who presented a paper at the Propulsion Workshop entitled *Design and Simulation of a Tether Boost Facility for GEO, Lunar, and Mars Transport.* "Momentum exchange tethers allow momentum and energy to be transferred between objects in space. Electrodynamic tethers interact with the Earth's magnetosphere to generate power or propulsion."

Electrodynamic tethers have already been flight tested, and the concept has proven to be a viable technology. In fact, it is being considered as a means to counteract the slight aerodynamic drag on the International Space Station, reducing the need for reboosts that rely on conventional chemical propellants. Such a system could possibly save the program about a billion dollars in operating costs over the life of the station . . .

Both types of tethers promise to reduce the cost of getting satellites into orbit and keeping them there or removing them.

"Right now if you needed to get a big payload out to geosynchronous orbit, you might need a $200 million rocket," said Hoyt, "but using a [momentum-exchange] tether system you could maybe do it with a $20 million rocket."

In one variant of a momentum-exchange tether, the faster-moving tether system grabs a slower-moving satellite in a lower orbit using a grapple at the end of a tether line between 20 and 200 kilometers long.

After orbiting around the Earth once together, the rotating tether system tosses the satellite forward into a higher orbit, somewhat like a roller derby skater grabbing a teammate and slinging them forward. The first skater transfers some of their momentum to the second skater, leaving the first skater going slower afterward. Similarly, the tether system gives some of its momentum to the satellite, ending up in a lower orbit.

The momentum-exchange tether then needs a way to return to its original orbit so that it can grab the next satellite.

In current designs, the momentum-exchange tether system will get the push it needs by acting as the other kind of tether—a conducting electrodynamic tether.

Electrodynamic tethers are typically between five and 20 kilometers long. As the long wire moves through Earth's magnetic field, the changing magnetic field in the vicinity of the wire induces a current that flows up the tether. If a power supply is added to the tether system and used to drive current in the other direction, an electrodynamic tether can "push" against the Earth's magnetic field to raise the spacecraft's orbit. The major advantage of this technique compared to other space propulsion systems is that it doesn't require any propellant.

The momentum gained by these tether systems is ultimately taken from the rotational momentum of the Earth.

"You're actually transferring the rotational momentum of the Earth to the satellite," said Kirk Sorensen, an aerospace engineer involved with momentum-exchange tether research at NASA's Marshall Space Flight Center in Huntsville, Alabama. "You're spinning down the Earth."

However, since the mass of the Earth is so many times greater than the satellite, the impact on the Earth's rotation is infinitesimal, Sorensen noted.

Electrodynamic tethers can be used as a brake as well as an accelerator.

If a current is not forced down the tether, the motion of the tether through the Earth's magnetic field will create a current traveling upwards. This produces a force that slows the system down rather than speeding it up.

Slowing a satellite down renders it unable to circle the Earth fast enough to "beat" gravity and so it falls back into the atmosphere. Without heat shielding, it will burn up.

Installing such a "suicide" device on satellites is actually more useful than it may sound.

"Commercial satellite companies have already recognized that if they leave the satellites up there, pretty soon they're going to get in the way of the other satellites that they want to put up," Hoyt said. Without one of these electrodynamic "brakes," an expired satellite can take months or years to fall out of orbit.

As elegant and useful as space tethers might someday be, however, the technology isn't ready for the big time yet.

"There are a few open issues preventing this from becoming a routinely usable technology," said Dr. Nobie H. Stone, a senior scientist at MSFC.

One question is the long-term survival of the tethers. While the atmosphere at Low Earth Orbit (LEO) altitudes is extremely thin—millions of times thinner than the air at sea-level—it is largely composed of atomic oxygen, which is very corrosive.

High-velocity micro-meteorites pose an even more recalcitrant problem. Exactly how to protect the thin tether material of electrodynamic tethers from small grains traveling at tens to hundreds of thousands of miles per hour is not clear.

"I don't think we have a good handle on that problem," Stone said.

Dr. Robert Forward, vice-president of Tethers Unlimited, noted that his company is working on a momentum-exchange tether design that uses redundant, interconnected lines to give the tether a high tolerance for micro-meteorite impacts.

Courtesy of NASA.

Ever since the dawn of the space age, we have become accustomed to seeing rockets shoot off into space. But many other exotic ideas for space travel will work as long as they adhere to Newton's second law of motion. This law states that any object with a force acting on it will undergo a net acceleration of its motion, thus illustrating the concept of conservation of energy and momentum.

Conservation of energy and momentum is also the principle behind solar sails. Solar sails are sails attached to spacecraft that are designed to convert light energy—in this case the photons streaming from the Sun or a laser pointed from Earth—into motion to propel the spacecraft to the farthest reaches of the universe. A solar sail combines all the forces acting upon it in such a way as to produce a net acceleration in the desired direction of travel. The energy comes from the momentum of the photons streaking across space at the speed of light. Such a gentle force from the Sun or a laser is perpetual and continuously accelerates the sail in space, making long-distance interstellar travel feasible.

*In "Solar Sail Technology Development,"
Dr. Deborah J. Jackson looks at the technology
behind solar sails and shows how scientists are
using the principle of the conservation of
energy and momentum in this unprecedented
way. —RV*

From "Solar Sail Technology Development"
by Dr. Deborah J. Jackson
NASA.gov, March 22, 2002

Solar sails are composed of large flat smooth sheets of
very thin film, supported by ultra-lightweight structures.
The side of the film which faces the sun is coated with
a highly reflective material so that the resulting product
is a huge mirror, typically about the size of a football
field. The force generated by the sun shining on this
surface is about equal to the weight of a letter sent via
first class mail. Even though this is a very tiny force, it
is perpetual, and over days, weeks, and months, this
snail-paced acceleration results in the achievement of
velocities large enough to overtake and pass the
Voyagers and *Pioneers* that are now speeding away
through the outer reaches of our solar system.

NASA has a program in place to develop solar sail
technology to a point where it can be used to implement
important space exploration missions. There are a
number of missions on the NASA strategic roadmap
that require this type of propellantless propulsion to
achieve their objectives. There are other classes of
missions that are greatly enhanced by solar sails

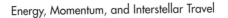

because these vehicles are inexpensive to construct and can deliver such high performance propulsion.

There are important applications for solar sails beyond the science missions that NASA has planned. The National Oceanic and Atmospheric Administration (NOAA) needs this technology to create a new class of space and earth weather monitoring stations that can provide greater coverage of the earth and provide more advanced warning of the solar storms that sometimes plague communications and electrical power grids. There are also a number of military missions in earth orbit that can be enabled by low cost sailcraft.

What Is Solar Sailing?

Solar sailing is a method of converting light energy from the sun into a source of propulsion for spacecraft. In essence, a solar sail is a giant mirror that reflects sunlight in order to transfer the momentum from light particles (photons) to the object one is interested in propelling. Since the phrase "solar sails" is often confused with "solar cells," which is a technology for converting solar light into electrical energy, we will use the term "light sail" for the purpose of this discussion.

The first suggestion that this energy could be harnessed for propulsion came nearly 400 years ago when astronomer Johannes Kepler observed comet tails being blown by what appeared to be a solar breeze. Believing that this was evidence that winds blew objects about in intrastellar space, he suggested that eventually ships might be able to navigate through space using sails fashioned to catch this wind. It is now widely recognized that because space is a vacuum, winds of any significance do not exist. What Kepler observed was the pressure of solar photons on dust particles that are released by the comet as it is orbiting. Photonic pressure is a very gentle force which is not observable on earth because the frictional forces in the atmosphere are so much larger. Thus, we only expect to observe and harness the force due to the pressure of light in the vacuum of space.

How Sails Work

We begin by explaining Newton's Second Law, $F = ma$, which says that any object with unbalanced forces acting to it, will under go a net acceleration of its motion. The principle behind harnessing a natural force, such as the wind or photons, lies in designing a craft which combines all the forces acting upon it in such a way as to produce a net acceleration in the desired direction of travel. Since there is an analogy between using a light sail to maneuver a space craft and a wind sail to maneuver a sail boat, the next section first discusses the more familiar wind sail, before introducing the force concepts that govern movement of the light sail.

Wind Sailing

. . .The hull . . . experiences a net force due to the flow of current in the ocean water. Consequently, in the absence of any other forces, the boat will tend to move naturally along the direction of the current flow. When powered by a sail, the boat will be subjected to a more complex set of forces. For example, the force applied to

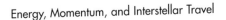

the main sail by the wind will be counter balanced by the force of the water against the centerboard. One controls the direction that the boat is pointing by using the rudder to introduce a drag on either side of the boat.

The net force of the wind splits between the front and back of the sail to produce a low pressure on the front of the sail foil and pull the boat forward. Changing the angle of the centerboard with respect to the direction of the wind changes the dynamics of the applied force. By balancing the forces acting on a sail boat, it is possible to execute the following three basic maneuvers: reaching, running, and tacking.

- Reaching—This is the ability to sail in directions that are near tangential to the direction of the wind. To reach, the centerboard is offset at an angle 90 degrees into the wind, and the sail is angled slightly off the centerboard to catch wind while also providing a forward thrust to the boat. A net positive force is then produced along the direction of the centerboard when the wind splits around both the front and back of the sail foil to produce a low pressure in the forward direction.

- Running—This is simply sailing along the direction of the wind, hence the sail is set about 90 degrees to the wind and the centerboard is set 180 degrees into the wind. Note that with no counterbalancing force from the water acting on the centerboard, maneuvering from this position tends to be unstable.

• Tacking—This is the art of sailing against the wind. The centerboard is offset at a small angle (up to 45 degrees into the wind). The combination of the water acting on the centerboard and the wind acting on the sail result in a net force along the centerboard which moves the boat at an angle against the wind. Most sail boats cannot sail closer than 45 degrees against the wind.

Battle of the Forces of Nature: Wind Vs. Photon Fluxes

As an example of the magnitude of the forces that the ancient Egyptians were able to harness by using kites to move massive stones, researchers recently demonstrated that they could use a wind sail (40.2 square meters in area) and wind gusts of 12 to 18 MPH to lift a large obelisk (mass = 15,200 kg) off the ground. If the acceleration due to gravity is 10 m/s/s, then the total force supplied by the sail was 1.52×10^5 Newtons . . .

At Earth's distance from the sun, the solar flux . . . in space is about 1.4 kilowatts per square meter. This is enough power to run a hair dryer continuously, but not enough to power a car . . .

For a 40.2 square meter sail similar to that used to raise the obelisk, the light force is only about 3.8×10^{-4} Newtons. Consequently, the pressure from the sun is roughly nine orders of magnitude weaker than what we can harness from the wind on the surface of the Earth. This force is so gentle that it would be completely swamped by atmospheric friction and is hence unnoticeable in our day to day activities.

On Earth, the Wind Wins!!

But in the vacuum of space, the tables are turned and the wind becomes the weakling. Because space is a vacuum the source of frictional drag disappears. Space is also very large, so it is easy to imagine building larger structures, kilometers on a side, to harness the force due to light pressure. There are still some particles (mostly charged residue ejected from the sun) blowing around as part of the solar wind, but their density is so low that the gentle force from the solar photon flux dominates by a factor of 1,000. Consequently: IN SPACE PHOTONS WIN!!

Solar Sailing—Acceleration Due to Gravity

Before we can explore the motion of a spacecraft with a light sail attached to it, we must first understand its natural motion in the presence of the sun's gravitational field. If one places a spacecraft in orbit around the sun, it moves on a trajectory that is defined by the sum of all the forces acting on it. The dominant force acting on an orbiting spacecraft is the centripetal force due to the gravitational pull of the sun . . . This force is balanced by the outward centrifugal force . . . of the spacecraft's motion.

Note that the spherical nature of the gravitational force means that the sail's angular setting will be very different from that observed with the sail boat . . .

Newton's Third Law

Newton's third law states that for every action, there is an equal and opposite reaction. One can observe this effect by tilting the solar sail so that its surface is no longer normal to the incident photons. Then the momentum component of the photon flux, which is parallel to the direction of motion, translates into a change in the tangential velocity . . .

If the photons are reflected along the direction of the spacecraft's motion, the imparted momentum pushes the spacecraft both outward from the sun as well as applying a decelerating force along its tangential direction of motion. It could be said that this is the light sail version of tacking because the spacecraft moves opposite the direction of the applied outward photon pressure.

The other maneuver of interest occurs when the mirror is tilted so that photons are reflected behind the trajectory. This imparts a forward momentum to the spacecraft, causing it to spiral outward . . . Now that you understand how to maneuver with light sails, you are ready to practice for the Solar Cup races . . .

Laser Assisted Light Sailing

Light sailing works well for inner planet missions and for activities extending out to the Mars orbit. However, the solar flux falls off as the inverse square of the distance from the sun. Thus for missions beyond the Jupiter orbit, an alternative to solar propulsion is to use directed light from a high power laser. As a pioneer inventor in the field of interstellar propulsion, Robert Forward has an avid interest in developing methods for boosting the intensity of light that can be delivered to a light sail. His goal is to reduce the cruise duration of a trip from our solar system to the nearest star from 6,500 years to a time frame on the order of 40 years . . .

Although the photon pressure is a comparatively gentle force, there is strong motivation to develop light sails that harness this force because it does not have to be carried as part of the payload of the spacecraft. It is a freebie from nature. Unlike chemical thrusters which apply short powerful thrusts to the spacecraft, which then coasts to its destination, solar propulsion is continuously applied. This leads to two important ramifications:

- Over time, the net force applied by the light sail exceeds what can be obtained using chemical propulsion.
- Continuous thrust means that course corrections can be applied more frequently, thereby opening up more trajectory options for any given mission.

[Four] main mission scenarios have been proposed for the use of light sails:

- Small solar kites (several meters in diameter) to replace the attitude control thrusters.
- Large light sails (100×100 m^2) for propulsion and maneuvering on inner planet missions.

- Larger light sails (200x200 m²) for outer planet missions.

- Super light sails (1000x1000 m²) for interstellar missions. Instead of using solar power, the light sail would be propelled by a 65 GW laser system.

Recently, C. Jack and <u>C.S.</u> Welch proposed using a solar kite, which is essentially a small light sail (approximately 3x3 m²) that can be used for attitude control. Indeed, a small "kite" or solar sail (31 cm x 76 cm in area) was actually added to the Mariner series of spacecraft to balance the solar pressure on the solar cells. However, it wasn't until the Mariner 10 mission that solar sailing techniques were used for maneuvering by using the pressure of sunlight reflecting off of the solar panels for attitude control. By using the ballast solar sail for attitude control maneuvering, the project was able to extend the planned life of the mission to get more data . . .

Design & Construction

There are three major designs used for light sail construction:

- Three axis stabilized sails which require booms to support the sail material.

- Heliogyro sails, which are bladed like a helicopter and must be rotated for stability.

- Disc sails which must be controlled by moving the center of mass relative to the center of pressure.

A practical sail places great demands on our physical construction capabilities. The sail must be as large as possible so that it can collect enough light to gain a useful thrust. At the same time it must be as lightweight as possible. This implies a very, very thin sail film with minimal mass. Finally, it must be durable enough to withstand a wide range of temperature changes, charged particles, and micrometeoroid hazards.

Materials Construction

The light sail material must be as thin and lightweight as possible. Conventional light sail film has comprised 5 micron thick aluminized mylar or kapton with a thin film aluminum layer (approximately 100 nm thick) deposited on one side to form a mirror surface with 90 % reflectivity. One of the more important sail film figures of merit is the areal density . . . From the areal density, one can calculate acceleration due to the solar light pressure at Earth orbit (1 AU) . . .

For 5 micron thick mylar, which has an areal density of 7 g/m^2, the acceleration would be 1.2 mm/s^2. This acceleration results in a daily velocity increase of about 100 m/s, a velocity which is useful for maneuvering around the solar system. Although mylar is inexpensive and readily available in 0.5 micron thickness, it is not the ideal sail film material because it is easily degraded by the sun's ultraviolet radiation. The other key contender, kapton, . . . is useful for a limited number of inner solar system missions, and is unacceptable for sail missions to the outer planets. Another interesting figure of merit for comparing solar sails is the achievable terminal velocity.

The terminal velocity expression suggests that the closer one can get to the sun for a gravity assisted maneuver, the higher a terminal velocity the solar sail can obtain . . . Consequently, the closest distance of approach before the solar sail melts limits the achievable terminal velocity.

Initial approaches for improving sail acceleration failed to take this into account because they focused only on developing the lowest density film material possible . . . More recently, nanotubes, a meshwork of interlocking carbon fibers which can provide stiff, but extremely lightweight support for the sail coating are being explored. Since the carbon is relatively impervious to solar-radiation damage and has a higher melting point than aluminum, the nanotubes are thought to have high potential for providing a significant breakthrough for light sail development; potentially yielding factors of 10,000 to 100,000 in Earth orbit acceleration. One concept, gray sails, tries to turn the tables on the heating problem by moving within 3 solar radii to heat the sail up to 2,000 degrees centigrade. The radiating heat would then act as a propellant as the spacecraft passes through perihelion and arcs away from the sun.

Courtesy of NASA.

Conservation on the Subatomic Level

2

Physicists believe that the nuclei of atoms rotate only when the distribution of mass or electric charge within the nucleus becomes unbalanced. This alters the path of the electrons, which are the negatively charged particles that orbit the nucleus. This imbalance, in turn, gives angular momentum to the nucleus. Following the principle of the conservation of momentum, the nucleus, in other words, spins.

By studying how nuclei spin, scientists can learn how to alter their spin within individual atoms. This type of research could have a practical payoff, leading to so-called molecular-cascade memory, an innovative type of memory chip that could pack data within individual atoms. This technology could ultimately lead to quantum computers, which could perform calculations millions of times faster than today's most advanced supercomputers.

Even computer giant IBM is taking advantage of this new technology. IBM's goal is to develop technology that can store as much memory as *possible within the smallest amount of space. This, in fact, is part of the goal of all computer companies because with ultimate memory storage, anything is technologically possible. And IBM reached for this goal by developing a measuring device designed to study the switching of the spin of individual atoms.*

An example of molecular-cascade memory that is available today in the form of Giant Magnetoresistive (GMR) spin-valve heads for magnetic hard-disk drives on computers. By controlling the spin of the electrons within these devices, the GMR head has allowed computers to be able to store forty times more information since this technology debuted in 1997.

In "A New Spin on Nuclei," Rod Clark and Bob Wadsworth explore how the age-old concept of the conservation of energy and momentum is being built upon to advance our understanding of the inner workings of subatomic particles. —RV

From "A New Spin on Nuclei"
by Rod Clark and Bob Wadsworth
Physics World, July 1998

The rotation of quantum objects has a long and distinguished history in physics. In 1912 the Danish scientist Niels Bjerrum was the first to recognize that the rotation of molecules is quantized. In 1938 Edward Teller and John Wheeler observed similar features in the spectra of excited nuclei, and suggested that this was caused by the nucleus rotating. But a more complete explanation had to wait until 1951, when Åage Bohr (the son of Niels) pointed out that rotation was a consequence of the nucleus deforming from its spherical shape. We owe much of our current understanding of nuclear rotation to the work of Bohr and Ben Mottelson, who shared the 1975 Nobel Prize for Physics with James Rainwater for developing a model of the nucleus that combined the individual and collective motions of the neutrons and protons inside the nucleus.

What makes it possible for a nucleus to rotate? Quantum mechanically, a perfect sphere cannot rotate because it appears the same when viewed from any direction and there is no point of reference against which its change in position can be detected. To see the rotation the spherical symmetry must be broken to allow an orientation in space to be defined. For example, a diatomic molecule, which has a dumbbell shape, can rotate about the two axes perpendicular to its axis of symmetry.

A quantum mechanical treatment of a diatomic molecule leads to a very simple relationship between rotational energy . . . and angular momentum . . .

These concepts can be applied to the atomic nucleus. If the distribution of mass and/or charge inside the nucleus becomes non-spherical then the nucleus will be able to rotate. The rotation is termed "collective" because many of the nucleons (the protons and neutrons) are involved. These nucleons follow well defined orbits inside the nucleus, just like electrons in an atom. The stability of a particular nucleus is closely related to the energies of these orbits . . . Small changes in the spatial alignment of these orbits lead to changes in the angular momentum (or spin) of the nucleus. Like molecules, nuclei have magnetic moments that are proportional to their angular momentum for a fixed configuration of nucleons.

Rotation in Nuclei

The most spectacular examples of collective rotation occur in "superdeformed" nuclei. These nuclei have ellipsoidal shapes in which the major axis is twice as long as the minor axis, like a rugby ball or an American football . . .

To populate the high angular momentum states in a nucleus, such as the superdeformed states, a thin metal foil is bombarded by high-energy ions. When a nucleus in the beam strikes a nucleus in the target foil, they can fuse together to create a "hot" compound nucleus. At first the nucleus loses energy by emitting light particles, such as neutrons, protons or alpha particles. Then, when its energy falls below the energy binding the particles together, it cools further by radiating gamma-rays. Since the energy levels of the deformed nucleus are regularly spaced, the gamma-rays form a characteristic "band" or "picket fence" spectrum. Only about 1% of the nuclei formed in these collisions go through a superdeformed stage.

The nucleus is thought to maintain its extreme shape as it loses angular momentum and energy. After

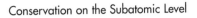

emitting approximately 10–20 gamma-rays the super-deformed nucleus, which is still highly excited, decays into states associated with a near-spherical shape that have about the same angular momentum but much less energy. The final decay process between these two shapes is still only partially understood.

A superdeformed nucleus emits electric quadrupole radiation . . . To think of this classically, imagine a metal rugby ball that is charged, spinning on its short axis. When either end of the ball is pointing towards an observer, the electromagnetic field is stronger than when a side of the ball faces the observer. Therefore, the field oscillates twice for every complete revolution of the rugby ball. A superdeformed nucleus spins incredibly quickly, about 10^{21} times per second, and by the time it has decayed to the ground state, the nucleus will have completed more revolutions than the Earth has done since it was formed.

Patterns of gamma-rays from superdeformed nuclei were first identified in 1986 at the Daresbury Laboratory in the UK in a collaborative project headed by Peter Twin of Liverpool University. Since then, powerful new spectrometers have been built to detect weak gamma-ray decay, including spectra from other examples of superdeformed nuclei. The latest generation of large detector arrays include "Euroball," which has been built by a collaboration of 30 nuclear physics groups in Europe, and "Gammasphere" in the US. Euroball was designed to be moved to various nuclear physics facilities in Europe and is currently at the

Legnaro National Laboratory in Italy. Gammasphere moved from the Lawrence Berkeley National Laboratory to the Argonne National Laboratory earlier this year.

Rethinking the Nucleus

Until recently it was thought that near-spherical nuclei always emitted irregular patterns of gamma-rays. However, in the early 1990s very regular patterns of gamma-rays—and hence possible evidence for rotation—were detected from nuclei that were known to be almost perfect spheres. Working independently, teams from York University in the UK, the Lawrence Berkeley and Lawrence Livermore National Laboratories in the US, and Bonn University in Germany found such patterns in the gamma-ray spectra of lead nuclei with mass numbers of 198 and 199. Similar examples have since been observed in isotopes of lead with mass numbers of between 191 and 202.

Detailed investigation yielded further surprises. The angular distribution and polarization of the gamma-rays showed that they were not electric quadrupole (E2) in nature but magnetic dipole (M1). Classically, M1 radiation is emitted from a rotating current loop, with the field oscillating at the same frequency as the frequency of rotation. Similar gamma-ray bands have recently been identified in cadmium, indium, tin and antimony nuclei in the mass region around 110, where the nuclei are also near-spherical. These spectra have a pattern that is typical of rotation, which poses an awkward problem: how can we explain these regular patterns of M1 gamma-rays?

In 1993 Stefan Frauendorf of the Centre for Nuclear and Hadron Research in Rossendorf, Germany, suggested that the patterns were due to a new mode of behaviour inside the nucleus. He proposed that most of the angular momentum of the nucleus could be generated by just a few of the protons and neutrons. In the case of lead-199, which has 82 protons and 117 neutrons, it is believed that most of the angular momentum comes from just two protons and three neutrons, with the remaining nucleons being passive observers. (Strictly speaking this angular momentum is carried by protons and "neutron holes." A neutron hole is the absence of a neutron, similar to an electron hole in a semiconductor.) Since only a few protons and neutrons are involved, there must be a very large angular momentum associated with their orbits.

The coupling of such orbits is governed by the overlap of the wavefunctions that represent the distribution of nucleon density in the nucleus. The protons are thought to have a toroidal (doughnut-shaped) density distribution, whereas the neutron holes have a dumbbell-shaped distribution. Generally, the configuration with the lowest energy is the one where the wavefunctions have the greatest overlap. In lead-199 this occurs when the angular momentum vectors of the protons and neutrons are perpendicular to each other. The alignment of these vectors relative to each other, and of the total angular momentum relative to the magnetic moment of the nucleus, changes during the de-excitation process.

The nuclei are created in highly excited energy and angular momentum states. For a fixed proton and neutron combination, the total angular momentum is at a maximum when the two vectors point in the same direction. During de-excitation these vectors gradually move apart from each other, and hence away from the total angular momentum vector . . . As the excess angular momentum and energy is carried away by gamma-rays, the nucleus approaches the minimum-energy configuration in which the two vectors are perpendicular and the overlap between the proton and neutron density wavefunctions is at a maximum. This process has been dubbed the "shears" mechanism because the motion of the proton and neutron angular momentum vectors resembles the opening of a pair of shears. As with superdeformed nuclei, only a small fraction of the nuclei (roughly 1–10%) are created in the shears mode.

A detailed theoretical treatment of the shears mechanism predicts that the "reduced transition probability" (which is inversely proportional to the lifetime of the states in the band) is proportional to the square of the component of the magnetic dipole moment of the nucleus . . . that is perpendicular to the total angular momentum vector. This component of the dipole moment is small when the angle between the neutron and proton angular momentum vectors is small. As the two vectors open, however, this component becomes larger and the reduced transition probability increases as the total angular momentum decreases. This prediction was recently confirmed by experiments using the Gammasphere array, putting the shears mechanism on a firm experimental footing.

It is easy to see how the orientation of a deformed nucleus (or a dumbbell diatomic molecule) can be specified. But it is not so easy to define an orientation for a nucleus displaying shears behaviour, for which the overall shape is near-spherical. To get a picture of the nucleus, consider the orbits of the few active protons and neutrons involved. Their configuration can be thought of as an anisotropic arrangement of crossed "current" loops embedded in the spherical mass distribution of the nucleus. (Neutrons possess an intrinsic magnetic moment even though they have no overall charge.) . . .

This behaviour has been termed "magnetic rotation" because the rotational sequences arise from the anisotropy of currents in the nucleus, which produce a magnetic moment. The more familiar rotation of deformed nuclei (and molecules) could be called "electric rotation" to reflect the fact that it results from an anisotropy in the charge distribution.

New Modes of Rotation

What might we expect from future studies of this new phenomenon? The highest priority is to find more examples of the shears mechanism, so that we can study it in a variety of nuclei. In widely separated mass regions the combination of protons and neutrons that form the "blades" of the shears will differ. Moreover, the core of the nucleus could assume different shapes. For example, the cases observed in the lead isotopes involve nuclei with small oblate deformations, whereas the examples in the tin region involve slight prolate deformations. And we have yet to find a case of "pure" magnetic rotation in a perfectly spherical nucleus. Another intriguing question is how and when the transition from magnetic to electric rotation occurs?

More exotic versions of the shears mechanism have also been predicted. For instance, both blades of the shears could be formed from the same type of particle (i.e. two neutron blades or two proton blades). However, such a combination could not give rise to a large magnetic dipole moment because the individual moments would be equal and opposite. A regular pattern of energy levels would still be formed from the opening shears, but the decay would now occur by weak electric quadrupole transitions. This has been termed "antimagnetic" rotation in analogy with antiferromagnetism.

Another possible shears mode could occur if the blades close with decreasing excitation energy rather than open. There is no physical reason to exclude this possibility, although it would be energetically unfavourable because the angular momentum would increase as the excitation energy is decreased. Again the result would be a regular pattern of energy levels. Researchers are currently devising experiments that could reveal these curious modes of behaviour.

The study of rotational motion in nuclear science and other branches of physics is currently an intensely active area of research. For example, rotational-like behaviour has even been observed in the excitation spectra of some families of elementary particles, which offers clues about the behaviour of the constituent quarks. Whatever is found in future studies, one thing is clear—the study of the rotational behaviour of quantum systems will continue to turn up surprises.

Reprinted with permission from *Physics World*.

In nuclear fusion, in which the nuclei of two atoms fuse together and release energy, mass and energy must be conserved. The total budget of mass and energy combined must be the same before and after the fusion reaction. If the mass is less after the reaction than before it, that mass must have been converted into energy.

As an example, the mass of a helium nucleus formed by fusing two hydrogen nuclei together is less than the mass of the two hydrogen nuclei before the reaction started. In this case, mass and energy are conserved by converting some of the mass into energy particles, otherwise known as photons.

In the fusion process, a relatively small amount of mass is converted into a tremendous amount of energy. Fusion provides a limitless number of energy resources. But in order to have a sustained fusion process, temperatures and pressures comparable to those found inside the Sun must be achieved here on Earth.

In "Fusion Energy: The Agony, the Ecstasy and Alternatives," John Perkins examines the

*new ways in which sustained fusion can be
achieved here on Earth, allowing us to convert
matter into energy efficiently for practical
energy sources. —RV*

"Fusion Energy: The Agony,
the Ecstasy and Alternatives"
by John Perkins
Physics World, November 1997

Most fusion research reactors confine the nuclear fuel
using magnetic fields. John Perkins argues that we
should not forget alternative methods, and calls for a
diversified world fusion programme.

Fusion—the release of nuclear binding energy from
light nuclei and its practical exploitation—has been a
major world research discipline for the past four
decades. It promises to be an energy resource capable of
indefinitely sustaining humanity under all conceivable
scenarios of population growth and energy demand. In
fact, fusion is the only energy source indigenous to
Earth that will last as long as our planet exists.

That's the ecstasy, so what's the agony? The problem
is that although we have made enormous progress in
our scientific understanding of fusion, we have, as yet,
no clearly identified route to an attractive commercial
fusion power plant that will sell in the energy marketplace of the 21st century and beyond.

Arguably, this situation has been exacerbated by the
fact that the world's fusion community has prematurely

concentrated on a single route to fusion power. This route is the conventional tokamak, in which magnetic fields are used to confine the nuclear fuel. Moreover, because we are still at a relatively early stage of fusion development, it is essential to strive for a diversified programme that can withstand the physics and technological uncertainties that accompany any single class of fusion-reactor concepts.

People often ask whether we will actually need fusion energy in the next century. Here at least there is an answer. Electrical power generation in the 21st century will be an industry worth tens of trillions of dollars, and there will be an assured and significant growth in demand from the developing world. The question really is whether we will have a fusion-reactor product that will be sufficiently attractive to compete in this marketplace. If we do, then fusion will be "needed."

The future viability of fusion energy therefore comes down to the question of the competition. So what else is out there? In the near term, the answer will continue to be fossil fuels in general, and natural gas in particular. However, once our access to such fossil fuels is foreclosed due to either exhaustion, environmental constraints or sequestering for other, more critical needs, there will remain only two indigenous energy sources that can fully sustain humanity for the foreseeable future. These are fission and fusion. Although renewable energy sources, such as solar power, will undoubtedly play important niche roles in the next century, they will not be able to sustain the central baseload demands of future society.

Fission Vs. Fusion

So how does our ultimate conception of a fusion reactor compare with fission? Both fission and fusion are forms of nuclear energy, but they can be differentiated by various attributes, including their capital costs, safety, environmental impact, proliferation problems and fuel availability. If the presently known reserves of fission fuels were used to sustain the full electrical energy needs of future populations, these fuels would probably not last for more than about 100 years using conventional thermal reactors with a "once-through" fuel cycle. However, such reserves could be made to last for thousands of years if they were efficiently used in breeder reactors with a reprocessed-fuel cycle. Uranium could also, in principle, be extracted from sea water, although we do not yet have the technology to achieve this.

In contrast, lithium—the primary fuel for "first-generation" deuterium-tritium fusion reactors—is significantly more abundant in the Earth's crust than either of the primary fission fuels, uranium or thorium. Lithium is also about 50 times more abundant than uranium in sea water. And deuterium, which is arguably the ultimate fusion fuel for "second-generation" deuterium-deuterium fusion, comprises 0.015 % of all of the hydrogen on Earth by atomic ratio. Thus, (deuterium) fusion is a fuel reserve that will be available to us for as long as the Earth exists.

What about the relative safety of fusion and fission power? The stored energy in the fuel of a fission core is sufficient for about two years of operation. So although adequately safe fission reactors probably can be designed, this stored energy could trigger severe accidents. In contrast, the amount of fuel in the core of a fusion reactor—of whatever class that we can conceive of today—is sufficient, at most, for only a few seconds of operation. The fuel would also be continually replenished.

The other disadvantage of fission is that spent fuel rods in a fission core contain gigaCuries of radioactivity in the form of fission products and actinides, some with half-lives of hundreds or even millions of years. Such radionuclides therefore have to be disposed of into securely guarded repositories deep underground. In contrast, the main potential for generating radioactive waste from fusion comes from neutron activation of the structural materials that surround the reactor. A judicious choice of these materials can reduce fusion's potential biological hazard by many orders of magnitude relative to spent fission fuel. Indeed, such materials would not need to be disposed of in a long-term waste repository.

Perhaps most importantly, we must recognize that the exploitation of breeder reactors to extend the fission fuel reserves of uranium and/or thorium beyond the next century will result in significant reprocessing traffic of 239Pu and/or 233U. Although international safeguards and security could no doubt be implemented, the diversion and exploitation of even a few kilograms of these materials would be a severe test of the public's stamina for this energy source.

Can Tokamaks Work?

To what extent do fusion's tangible advantages compensate for the present perceived disadvantages of the cost and complexity of the fusion reactor core? I believe that this question has not yet been fully addressed— either by the world fusion community or by its detractors. In fact, it cannot be satisfactorily answered until our physics research programmes have matured enough to identify the path to a tangible commercial-reactor product. We have made tremendous scientific progress in the world fusion programme over the past 40 years. That is incontrovertible. Our basic understanding of the rich and complex phenomena underlying plasma physics has increased profoundly, as has our ability to control these processes to our ends. In particular, our achievement of the basic "figure of merit" for magnetic-confinement fusion—the product of the plasma density, energy confinement time and plasma temperature—has increased by around six orders of magnitude over this period. It is now approaching the value required to realize a self-sustaining ignited burn in a mixture of deuterium and tritium fuel, in which no external energy would be required.

To date, most of the world's fusion research funds have been spent on the tokamak approach. Because of the tokamak's capacity for holding heat and its effectiveness in achieving the required magnetic-field configuration, it has proved to be the best research tool so far for achieving fusion conditions in the laboratory. For example, the Joint European Torus (JET) tokamak at

Culham in the UK should soon approach—and hopefully exceed—"scientific break-even," at which the fusion energy output exceeds the external energy injected to drive the reaction. Despite the pulsed fusion devices that demonstrated (perhaps unfortunately for humanity) extremely high fusion gains in the early 1950s, this will be a unique and exciting achievement for thermonuclear fusion research.

So we have some confidence that the tokamak can conceivably produce a fusion power reactor that works. For these reasons, the International Thermonuclear Experimental Reactor (ITER) project—a multi-billion dollar international engineering design study of a burning fusion plasma experiment—has focused on the tokamak as its vehicle of choice. However, it is not clear that the conventional tokamak approach will lead to a practicable commercial power plant that anyone will be interested in buying. This is a consequence of its projected low power density, high capital cost, high complexity and expensive development path. After all, the acid test for fusion energy is, ultimately, not its scientific achievements but whether it will be adopted by the market. Certainly, the tokamak is a valuable scientific research tool for studying high-temperature plasma physics and it must continue to be supported to that end. However, such support should not—and must not—come at the exclusion of other, potentially viable routes.

Alternative Options

The main alternative to the tokamak in the world fusion energy programme is the stellarator, and there are vigorous research programmes on this concept in both Europe and Japan. However, I believe that in the future, companies that are looking to build electricity generating plants that are cost-effective and reliable will view a fusion reactor based on the stellarator as being no different to that based on the tokamak. In other words, we must acknowledge that the tokamak and stellarator are two closely related approaches that belong to the same class of fusion concepts. If the tokamak ultimately turns out to be too expensive and complex to engineer—and so fails the commercial reactor test—then so might the stellarator.

These future uncertainties are best addressed by broadening our range of approaches. I believe that at this formative stage of fusion research it is too early— and unnecessary—to put all our eggs in one basket. It is beyond the scope of this article to examine an exhaustive list of alternative fusion concepts but, fortunately, a number do exist at varying stages of maturity. Within magnetic-confinement fusion, the spherical torus, the spheromak and the field-reversed configuration could lead to a much cheaper, more compact fusion-power core. These designs are certainly worth pursuing to the proof-of-principle stage. In particular, there is one class of fusion concepts—inertial fusion energy (IFE)—that can be considered a step change in their manner of realizing fusion energy.

In IFE, a millimetre-sized capsule of fusion fuel is compressed by an energetic pulse of energy from a "driver," which is typically a heavy-ion accelerator or a laser. The drive energy is delivered in a precise way to cause the fuel capsule to implode, creating—during the short inertial time before the target flies apart—the high densities and temperatures necessary for fusion to occur.

Although both magnetic and inertial fusion are at about the same stage of scientific understanding, the scientific and technological criteria by which these two distinct approaches will succeed or fail are very different. In particular, IFE provides a route to a fusion power plant that is a paradigm shift away from that of a tokamak and indeed from that of all other fusion concepts of the magnetic-confinement class. It offers, I believe, the potential for lifetime fusion chambers with renewable liquid coolants facing the targets, instead of solid, vacuum-tight walls that would be damaged by heat and radiation.

Protected in this way, all of the reactor structural materials would be lifetime components, and their minimal residual radioactivity would mean that at the end of the fusion plant's life, the materials could be buried on-site and near the surface, rather than deep underground. The use of such thick liquid protection would probably also eliminate the need for an expensive R&D programmes on exotic, low-activation materials. Moreover, IFE plants are inherently "modular," in that several, independent fusion chambers could be constructed around a single driver. This provides operational redundancy, in that one chamber could be shut down for maintenance while the others are up and running. This also provides the option that the plant could be expanded in phases to match any growth in demand. These are both important characteristics for future multi-GWe electrical reservations.

Our scientific understanding of inertial-confinement fusion should also be significantly advanced early in the next century by the completion and operation of the National Ignition Facility (NIF) at the Lawrence Livermore National Laboratory in the US, and the Laser Megajoule (LMJ) facility in France. Indeed, the NIF may be the first laboratory device to realize fusion "ignition." This is the process whereby the energy deposited by energetic alpha particles from the deuterium-tritium fusion reaction promotes a self-sustaining burn in the surrounding fuel, resulting in significant fusion energy gain.

Although the primary missions of both the NIF and the LMJ are defence related, a spin-off benefit of the NIF—and presumably the LMJ—is to show that inertial-fusion energy is feasible. Of course, much parallel work still needs to be done so that these demonstrations can be converted into the technical and economic success of an inertial-fusion power plant. In particular, today's lasers are not suitable for power-production applications, and the development of a suitable and cost-effective driver is the decisive research area.

Heavy-ion accelerators are attractive candidates for IFE because they build on our extensive experience with high-energy and nuclear physics facilities. They also promise efficiency, long life and magnetic final optics—whereby the beam is focused onto the target—that are relatively immune to the effects of the target explosions. Certainly, the high ion currents needed are a new and challenging element. Other candidate drivers include diode-pumped solid-state lasers as well as krypton fluoride lasers. The problem is that the development of IFE as a distinct class of alternative fusion concepts is not being pursued with the funding vigour that it deserves in the world fusion energy programme. Because of the long lead time required to bring a new energy technology to market, this situation must change if we are to provide society with the technical information necessary to pursue inertial-fusion energy to its full potential in the next century.

The Future for Fusion?

I believe that advances leading to a clearly economic fusion reactor lie in the parallel investigation of alternative approaches, rather than simply in engineering the nuts and bolts for the present conventional approach. This is particularly important for the US, where fusion research budgets have declined in recent years and where a fresh, vigorous rationale is required. The smartest investment of our world research budgets would be to press for innovation and understanding of the physics of various advanced concepts—this is, after all, where the greatest uncertainties lie, and where the greatest potential exists for improving the economics of the ultimate fusion power plant.

Alternative physics approaches are particularly important if we are ever to exploit the so-called "advanced" fusion fuels. Such fuels suggest several advantages over "conventional" deuterium-tritium reactions. For example, they produce few or even no neutrons, and they could even directly convert charged fusion products into electricity without the need for a conventional thermal cycle. However, such fuels would require significantly higher plasma densities and temperatures to realize the same fusion power density as deuterium-tritium plasmas.

As in cancer research, the world fusion programme has made enormous progress in the fundamental understanding of its field. But, again like cancer research, we have not yet arrived at our ultimate goal. Because of the profound benefit to future humanity of the ultimately successful end-point—a limitless energy source for all time—we must continue with an innovative and, most importantly, diverse fusion research programme until that goal is accomplished.

Reprinted with permission from *Physics World*.

If a nanomachine were scaled up to the size of a gumball, then a single red blood cell, by comparison, would be the size of a football stadium. Nanomachines could be used to construct and repair a variety of structures too small for us to otherwise work with. They could also potentially travel inside the human body. These machines will use mechanical energy, but they will need "nanomotors" to provide the energy to drive them.

Providing power at the nanoscale, however, where devices can consist of only a few molecules, poses daunting problems for engineers. Normal-scale machines simply feed off electricity from a copper wire or a combustion engine.

In experiments with nanotechnology, physicists have observed that when a small amount of tin (Sn) in crystal form is laid on a copper (Cu) surface, it appears to "skip" across the copper. The tin is converting chemical energy into forward motion, thus overcoming the friction between the tin and the copper surface by harnessing the benefits from the conservation of energy and momentum.

Though the researchers are impressed by the speed and efficiency of the process, harnessing this energy for chemical "motors" remains a challenge. It is hard to deliver energy, momentum, or angular momentum to nanosystems, since these systems cannot be well attached to external electrical or mechanical contacts. —RV

"How to Power a Nanomotor"
by Flemming Besenbacher and Jens K. Norskov
Science, **November 24, 2000**

Nanomotors are a particularly attractive goal for nanotechnology. Such nanometer-scale structures capable of converting chemical energy into work will be needed in many types of nanodevices, including switches, pumps, and actuators. To construct a nanomotor, we need to find ways of making nanostructures propel themselves and experimental methods that can track the motion.

The work of Schmid *et al.* can be viewed as a direct observation of a nanomotor (1). The authors find that nanoscale islands of tin deposited on a copper surface spontaneously move around on the surface, using the chemical energy released by alloying Sn into Cu (which is an exothermic chemical reaction) to overcome the friction between the Sn island and the Cu surface. The observations were made possible by applying two complementary experimental techniques, the scanning tunneling microscope (STM) (2) and the low-energy electron microscope (LEEM) (3), to obtain information about the atomic-scale structure as well as the motion of the islands on the surface.

Let alloy formation do the work. An Sn island skates around on a Cu(111) surface while exchanging Sn atoms for Cu atoms.

The development of the STM (2), in which a tip is raster-scanned across a surface and a small tunnel current (on the order of a nanoampere) is recorded in each pixel, has revolutionized the field of surface science, because it allows the structure of surfaces to be explored with unprecedented resolution. Direct real-space images of individual atoms and molecules on surfaces can now be obtained on a routine basis. Another very successful new microscope, the LEEM (3), exploits the wave nature of electrons that are scattered elastically from a surface. With this microscope, entities on the surface that are larger than 5 to 10 nanometers can be imaged and followed over time. The LEEM differs from conventional electron microscopes in that the electrons are of much lower energy (1 to 100 eV), enabling the LEEM to only observe surface features; the image contrast is based on diffraction of the electrons. The LEEM superbly supplements the STM, and in combination, the two techniques bridge the gap between mesoscopic and atomic-scale structures on surfaces.

Alloying in the first layer of a metal surface is vastly different from alloying in the bulk. In fact, a new type of two-dimensional alloy phase that only exists in the outermost surface layer has recently been discovered (4). Density functional calculations have provided a thorough database of phase diagrams that can be used to predict the existence of surface alloys (5). Metals that do not alloy in the bulk may alloy at the surface, and even for stable bulk alloys, there can be large differences in the stability of the bulk and the surface alloy. These new surface alloy phases open up new possibilities for designing materials with interesting physical and chemical properties (6).

The effect studied by Schmid *et al.* exemplifies some of the special properties of surface alloys. Just after deposition of Sn on a Cu(111) surface [where (111) denotes the exposure of the densest possible surface of the bulk material], the Sn atoms coalesce into large islands containing ~100,000 atoms. The alloying of Sn with Cu is an exothermic process, leading to the formation of a bronze (7), but the process is even more exothermic if Sn is in the topmost layer. Exchange between an Sn atom in the island and a Cu atom in the layer just underneath the island is therefore possible. It is more energetically favorable, however, if the island moves away from the location at which the exchange takes place. The island cannot move in a direction where exchange has already happened because it is repelled by the mixed phase, and therefore the Sn islands are constantly seeking out new areas on the surface that do not yet contain any Sn.

Only the combined use of the two powerful experimental techniques allowed Schmid *et al.* to study the needle in detail (the formation of the bronze alloy on the nanoscale) with the STM while at the same time keeping an eye on the haystack (the correlated motion of the Sn islands on the Cu surface on a mesoscopic scale) with LEEM. The experiments show in unprecedented detail how even a relatively simple system consisting of one metal deposited on another can exhibit very complex dynamics. One may envision using this nonrandom process as a mechanism for organizing nanoscale alloy structures over large length scales.

The system studied by Schmid *et al.* can be considered as a paradigm for a new class of nanomotors in which chemical energy is converted into work. In this case, the chemical energy released when the Sn is incorporated into the Cu surface (rather than into deeper layers) is converted into forward motion of the islands. According to density functional calculations, the energy released when an Sn atom is segregated from the second layer (below the Cu-Sn island) to the surface of Cu(111) is on the order of 1 eV (7). From the experiments, the Sn-Cu exchange rate is about one atom per 4000 s at room temperature. An island with 100,000 atoms will therefore release [an amount of horsepower (hp) that] implies that the power-to-weight ratio is roughly 0.3 hp/kg. For comparison, a car typically has 100 hp and a weight of 1000 kg, giving a similar power-to-weight ratio of 0.1 hp/kg.

The challenge is to devise nanomotors whose motion can be controlled externally (so that they can be used to move things around at will) and that can be refueled. These two requirements may be coupled if the availability of fuel can be controlled externally. The principle behind the Sn/Cu motor may be extended to the incorporation of molecules supplied from the gas phase through islands into a more stable compound in the surface.

References

1. A. K. Schmid, N. C. Bartelt, R. Q. Hwang, *Science* **290**, 1561 (2000).
2. G. Binnig, H. Rohrer, *Rev. Mod. Phys.* **59**, 615 (1987).
3. E. Bauer, *Surf. Sci.* **299/300**, 102 (1994).
4. L. Pleth Nielsen *et al.*, *Phys. Rev. Lett.* **71**, 754 (1993).
5. A. Christensen *et al.*, *Phys. Rev. B* **56**, 5822 (1997).
6. F. Besenbacher *et al.*, *Science* **279**, 1913 (1998).
7. A. Ruban, private communication.

The laws of energy and mass conservation are so simple, they can govern a huge variety of processes seen all the way from the behavior of atoms to the formation of galaxies. From this perspective, the universe is a grand laboratory for testing these conservation laws as they apply to some of the smallest things in nature: the subatomic particles that make up cosmic rays, and neutrinos, which are particles that weakly interact with matter.

Giant accelerators on Earth are used to study these particles by colliding atoms at high speeds, causing them to break apart into their constituent particles. The particles from a disassembled atom must obey conservation laws as observed in these collisions. For example, when a radioactive nucleus emits an electron, the electron may have any energy from zero up to a certain maximum. When the electron has less than the maximum possible value, the remaining energy must be carried away by another particle, called a neutrino. Physicists deduce that the charge must be zero, otherwise the law of conservation would be violated during the decay.

Space-based detectors offer a new opportunity to study particles from nature's own accelerators, including supernovas, black holes, and other energetic processes. Particles in the universe can be accelerated to near–light speed by black holes and neutron stars. These create a zoo of subatomic particles that can be observed *and tested against interactions observed in the laboratory.*

In "Fundamental Physics from Space and in Space," M. Jacob studies the ways in which subatomic particles can be studied using the fundamental principle of the conservation of energy and momentum. —RV

From "Fundamental Physics from Space and in Space"
by M. Jacob
Advances in Space Research, December 2003

The past twenty years have witnessed an increasing interest in particle physics related to space. A whole new field of investigation, "astroparticle physics," has been born. Many research organizations and funding structures have already taken this trend into account. This interest in particle physics from space may seem peculiar, since cosmic rays, which had long provided the only sources of very high energy particles, had been almost abandoned in the 1950s in favour of accelerators, which could give intense sources of high energy particles under specified conditions. Accelerators are now often operated as colliders reaching very high energies with high luminosity. These accelerators and colliders are wonderful tools . . .

Particle Physics with Accelerators and from Space

At present, the main "fundamental" trends in astroparticle physics are: 1) the study of cosmic rays, their composition and their very high energy spectrum; 2) the study of neutrinos at very high energies from distant cosmic sources and at lower energies from production in the upper atmosphere, from supernovae and from the Sun; 3) the search for exotic objects and for dark matter under different forms; 4) the detection of gravitational waves.

The Standard Model: Success and Questions

Progress in particle physics, through four decades of accelerator-based research, has led to a much better understanding of the structure of matter, revealing the quark structure and culminating in the Standard Model in a detailed and accurate description of all observed phenomena. We now have a good understanding of the quark and lepton structure of matter down to 10^{-18} m. Even more interesting, we have in this way reached a good understanding of the nature and of the origin of the fundamental interactions. While we still have many constituents to deal with, namely 3 doublets of quarks existing under 3 varieties of colours, and 3 doublets of leptons, we have a single gauge symmetry principle at the origin of all the fundamental interactions. These successes have opened deeper questions and also clues on how to attack longstanding puzzles. Crucial among the latter is the origin of mass . . .

Of key importance is the question of neutrino mass. If neutrinos have masses, albeit very small ones, they may change their nature revealing oscillations between neutrino species as they travel over macroscopic distances.

This is searched for with accelerators, but also underground detectors observing neutrinos from the Sun or produced at the top of the atmosphere. Soon we may combine the two with accelerators producing neutrinos and underground detectors detecting them thousands of kilometres away.

Particle Physics and Cosmology

Accelerator-based research has also advanced our understanding of the cosmos at large, especially of events just after the Big Bang. At the beginning, the temperature falls as the inverse square root of time. The prevailing physics is the high energy physics we know through accelerator research. For instance, with research at LEP we understand the dynamics of interactions in the Universe when it was 10^{-10} s old. With the LHC, we gain 2 orders of magnitude, reaching 10^{-12} s. Between these times, the Universe went through a transition with a dramatic change of phase of the vacuum. Its early thermal history is indeed rich in events which show carnages of particles and antiparticles leaving only a relatively small number of stable particles (one in a billion) as survivors. It is also rich in transitions through which the vacuum changed phase, thus breaking primordial symmetries present openly in the past but now hidden.

High energy physics has become an important element of cosmology. Understanding better the dynamics of the early Universe has in turn opened new and fascinating questions. We realize that the mass associated with visible stars is probably only a few percent of the total mass in the Universe. The search for "dark matter" has thus become a great challenge. There is the question of the neutrino mass and the related one of possible oscillations between neutrino species . . . There could also be some hitherto unknown particles, in particular high-mass ones, some left as stable relics of the Big Bang. Clues are looked for with accelerator physics but also from space. On accelerators, we look in particular for supersymmetric partners to the known particles. The LHC energy range should offer a most promising hunting ground.

The one of lowest mass could be one of the WIMPS (Weakly Interacting Massive Particles) looked for from the cosmos. At present cosmological models may favour a critical density with 30% of hot matter (neutrinos?) and 70% of cold matter (MACHO's and WIMP's beside the visible stars?). It is indeed likely that a large fraction, if not all, of the mass now ascertained in the halos of galaxies could be standard matter within non-shining objects (MACroscopic Halo Objects). They are searched for astronomically using gravitational lensing. The highly sophisticated data handling techniques borrow much from particle physics; this research is indeed carried to a large extent by particle physicists. Up to 15% of the critical density could be in such a hadronic form of matter, this being the maximum allowed by baryosynthesis and nucleosynthesis when the Universe was less than 200 s old.

The Big Bang was the most violent event ever, and could have produced massive particles which cannot yet be produced with accelerators. But the present

Universe, observed outside of the visible spectrum, also provides multiple examples of violent phenomena, producing very energetic particles. Studying such particles with particle physics techniques is providing most valuable astrophysics data. Neutrino physics, well understood through accelerator research, provides a precious though difficult way to study these phenomena on particles not affected by their long journey through space. One can thus also look into the interior of the more quiet stars.

Matter and Antimatter

The physical laws show a beautiful symmetry between matter and antimatter . . . It is tempting to assume such a symmetry between matter and antimatter at the level of the Universe, even if, in our neighbourhood, matter happens to prevail. However, as seen from the thermal history of the Universe, the Big Bang implies that all the antimatter, which was previously practically as abundant as matter, disappeared early . . .

Quarks and antiquarks, leptons and antileptons were initially in thermal equilibrium with photons. At present the cosmic microwave background contains a billion photons for each proton or electron seen. This tallies with the carnages of matter and antimatter that took place in the early Universe. If large amounts of antimatter were still annihilating against matter in the Universe this would lead to well-defined gamma-ray signals, not found up to the "local" supercluster level, which represents the largest known structure in the Universe at present . . .

Underground Research

. . . On the other hand, the question of supernova neutrinos, solar neutrinos, atmospheric neutrinos and very high energy neutrinos could come under study with fascinating results. At present, there seems to be a deficit of electron neutrinos from the Sun and of muonic neutrinos from the atmosphere, as if neutrinos of one kind transform themselves (oscillating) into neutrinos of another kind. This is a great result, but one still needs more statistics and more information on the energy of the capture neutrinos. Several underground (or underwater) detectors have been built, and more ambitious ones are being built or considered, for the primary role of studying cosmic neutrinos.

In Europe, there is the Italian-led Gran Sasso laboratory, already busy with many experiments; the Greek-led Nestor project, an underwater array off the coast of Greece; the Swedish-led project Amanda, deep under the South polar ice-cap, and several others of lesser importance. Other big international projects include: Homestake, IMB, DUMAND and the Solar-Neutrino Observatory in America; the Baksan underground laboratory in Russia; Kamiokande and SuperKamiokande in Japan.

The Study of Gravitation

The Standard Model still leaves gravity aside. Particle theorists are working hard to include it, with full legitimacy, in their global study of the basic interactions but have a long way to go. We are still far from a quantum theory of gravity, even if superstrings may perhaps provide insights on what the solutions would be. Valuable clues toward a more refined theory may come from ultra-precise experiments, in particular, tests of the Equivalence Principle. A deviation would put limits on the validity of Einstein's General Relativity. Within the theory, a very important step would be to collect direct evidence for gravitational waves. This is a challenging prospect. Ground studies of gravitational waves are going through an important development. In the framework of GR, gravitational waves should exist and the evolution of pulsar binaries, such as the famous Hulse Taylor one, fits the GR prediction very well. This can be considered as a proof, if still indirect, of gravitational radiation . . . This is the aim of the VIRGO project in Europe and the LIGO project in America. Coincidence measurements between interferometers (2 in America, 1 in Europe) should eventually detect radiation gravitational waves. Ground-based detectors are most efficient in the 10^2 to 10^3 Hz range but they are blind at low frequencies (<10 Hz) because of gravitational and thermal noise on the Earth. The higher frequency domain is where we expect signals from supernova collapse and from the end stage of compact binaries as they go through a final phase of chirp radiation, coalescence and ringdown. This is very interesting, but requires luck because of the not-so-probable occurrence of such events, even at a detection level corresponding to our nearby cluster of galaxies, Virgo. The value of h is proportional to the energy involved in the non-spherical part of the collapse and inversely proportional to the distance to the source. The signal from a supernova should be clear but it is hard to estimate since it depends on the particular nature of the collapse. For coalescence, one can match the signals to templates. Such signals come only once and are rather brief (fraction of a second to minutes); for them, coincidence techniques are essential. Signals from stable binaries, on the other hand, are continuous but being in the low-frequency range, require detection in space. So does the detection of very massive black holes . . .

Fundamental Physics in Space— Present Aspirations

One may try to anticipate what fundamental physics in space will look like up to two decades ahead using, as a guide, ESA's future long-range study. The sophistication and cost of the needed instruments are indeed such that long-range planning is essential.

In 1993, ESA made a Call for Mission Concepts in order to prepare its Horizon 2000+ programme, a rolling forward continuation of its Horizon 2000 programme as it had reached mid-term. The combination defines the key elements of space research in Europe up to 2020. The Call for Mission Concepts resulted in 110 proposals, close to 30 of which fell under the general heading of fundamental physics! Fundamental physics has many facets. Those, considered more particularly, fell under the headings of cosmology, gravitation and particle physics, microgravity experiments being reviewed separately, as something that should rather be linked with the Space Station . . .

Today . . . the detection of gravitational waves falls under fundamental physics. This is proper. We are not so much after the detection of gravitational waves, but the understanding of their properties and production, in particular, the high-field regime.

What is fundamental physics in space now? The best definition is a pragmatic one, according to the proposals received. They correspond to the wishes and aspirations of the community. The ESA Fundamental Physics Advisory Group identified six main fields: (i) tests of the Equivalence Principle [3 proposals], (ii) tests of Newton's law [2 proposals], (iii) particle physics [1 proposal on cosmic background neutrinos], (iv) gravitational waves [2 proposals], (v) search for long-range spin-dependent interactions [3 proposals], (vi) qualitative tests of Einstein's theory [10 proposals].

There were still other proposals, but of a more technological nature. Those were often aimed at testing new technologies needed for the realization of some of the scientific missions falling under these entries. Identifying so-called "enabling technologies" has indeed much to do with any recommendation.

Conclusion

Fundamental physics using cosmic sources offers many exciting prospects, whether on the ground or in space. In particular, the observation and study of gravitational waves appears at long last as within reach with a most interesting complementarity between ground-based and space-based detection. In particle physics, we are used to a long wait between dreams and reality; physics in space extends that further. So fascinating are the technical challenges and the spin-offs from developing the needed detectors, that we can still maintain enthusiasm for projects which will reach completion only 20 years from now.

Reprinted from *Advances in Space Research*, Vol. 32, by M. Jacob, "Fundamental Physics from Space and in Space," pp. 1197–1202, © 2003, with permission from Elsevier.

Planets, Moons, and Asteroids

3

Gravitational force weakens over distance. Tidal force is an effect of this difference in gravitational force from one side of a gravitationally affected body to another.

The term "tidal force" is referred to frequently when we talk about ocean tides. Ocean tides occur because the Moon is so close to Earth that its gravity pulls more strongly on the side of Earth facing the Moon than it does on the side facing away from it. This difference in gravitational force causes the Moon and the side of Earth facing the Moon to bulge like a stretched piece of taffy. As a result, the ocean level rises.

But the Moon's tidal influence is much more profound than the effect it has on rising and lowering sea levels. Because energy and momentum must be conserved, the tidal force that the Moon exerts on Earth is continuously driving the Moon away from Earth and slowing Earth's rotation. This discovery introduces scientists to a new example of how the conservation

*of energy and momentum appears in ways in
the universe that have never been seen
before.* —RV

From "Interplanetary Low Tide"
by Dr. Tony Phillips
NASA.gov, May 4, 2000

. . . Tides on our planet are caused by the gravitational
pull of the Moon and Sun. Earth's oceans "bulge out"
because the Moon's gravity pulls a little harder on one
side of our planet (the side closer to the Moon) than it
does on the other. The Sun's gravity raises tides, too, but
lunar tides are twice as big. When the Sun and the Moon
are approximately aligned (as they are when the Moon is
New or Full) we experience especially high tides called
"Spring Tides." When there is a 90-degree angle between
the two, we get lower tides called "Neap Tides."

Ocean tides on Earth can be as high as 12 meters
(40 ft) depending on local geography and the alignment of the Moon and Sun. Earth has solid ground
tides too, but they amount to less than 20 centimeters
(about 8 inches).

Although the Moon is small compared to behemoths
like the Sun and Jupiter, lunar tidal forces are dominant
because the Moon is so nearby. Tidal stretching is
proportional to the inverse cube of the distance to the
source of gravity. (If you moved the Moon to twice its
present distance, its tidal influence would decrease by
a factor of $2^3 = 8$). Thus, nearby objects—even small

ones like the Moon—raise high tides, while distant giants like Jupiter don't produce much of an effect.

"The force of Newtonian gravity falls off as the *square* of the distance," explains [University of Florida Department of Astronomy Professor George] Lebo, "but tidal forces decline as its *cube*. Tides are caused by gravity, so why aren't they the same? The reason is simply that tidal stretching comes from a difference in the gravitational pull felt on two sides of a body. In a $1/r^2$ gravitational field, the *difference in gravity between any two points* falls off as the cube of the distance, not the square."

After the Sun and the Moon, Venus is the object in our solar system that produces the biggest tides on Earth. This is simply because the Earth comes closer to Venus than any other planet. Even when the two are separated by their minimum distance of 0.3 AU, which happens every year and a half on average, Venus increases the size of our ocean tides by less than 0.005 cm. (Note: An AU, or "astronomical unit", is the distance between the Earth and the Sun. 1 AU = 1.5×10^8 km.)

Tides caused by the biggest planet in our solar system, Jupiter, are 10 times less than the ones we feel from Venus. Once again the reason involves distance. Although Jupiter is 388 times more massive than Venus, its closest approach to Earth is 14 times greater than our planet's minimum distance to Venus.

That's not to say that Jupiter isn't a powerful source of tides in its vicinity. You just have to be nearby to feel them. The innermost of Jupiter's big moons, Io, experiences tidal forces nearly 20,000 times stronger than the forces we feel here on Earth due to the Moon. Solid tidal bulges on Io are about 100m high, taller than a 40-story building! This stretching triggers some of the most active volcanoes in the solar system.

Courtesy of NASA.

Scientists aren't positive how Earth acquired the Moon. One explanation is that it was formed from a disk of dust and particles surrounding the young Earth that eventually came together. But where did this disk of debris come from? Earth could not have captured such space debris with its gravity alone.

This question leads to the speculation that the material that formed the disk came from Earth itself, blasted off our planet as a result of a giant impact with another celestial body such as an asteroid. But by calculating the conservation of energy and momentum, computer simulations show that the asteroid would have to be more than twice as massive as Mars, much larger than previously believed, in order to produce enough debris to form our moon.

In this article, using the principle of conservation of energy and momentum, Jack Lissauer attempts to solve the mystery of just where our moon came from. —RV

From "It's Not Easy to Make the Moon"
by Jack J. Lissauer
Nature, September 25, 1997

Theory has it that the Moon grew within a disk of material splashed out of the Earth by a body the size of Mars. According to new calculations, however, the impacting body was at least twice that size.

Earth's Moon is one of the most peculiar bodies in the Solar System. It is slightly more than 1 per cent as massive as the Earth, its primary, whereas (excluding the tiny Pluto-Charon "double planet") all other moons are less than one-fortieth of 1 per cent as massive as their primaries. Moreover, the Moon's composition is quite unusual—it is an extremely dry place, devoid of water and other volatile substances; yet it is anomalously low in density for a body in the inner Solar System, because it is depleted in iron relative to a solar-composition mix of refractory (high-condensation-temperature) elements.

Presumably, the satellites of the giant planets formed within disks of gas and dust orbiting their primary (as did the planets themselves, the primary in this instance, of course, being the Sun). But it is unclear how a solid planet such as Earth could acquire such a disk, so other models of lunar formation have been developed. Each, however, has had its drawbacks.

Was the Moon born from the Earth—that is, thrown off from a rapidly rotating young planet (the fission hypothesis)?[1] If most of Earth's iron had already settled into the core, this model could explain the

Moon's severe anaemia, but the dynamical aspects of the theory seem intractable.[2] Did the Moon grow from a disk of planetesimals captured into Earth's orbit (the coaccretion hypothesis)?[3] It appears unlikely that a solid planet would acquire a massive disk in such a manner, and this model does not account for the Moon's low iron content. Finally, was the Moon captured into orbit about the Earth, either intact or in fragments torn apart by Earth's tidal pull? This is unlikely according to dynamical calculations,[2] and such a model again doesn't explain the Moon's low abundance of iron, which is one of the most common elements that condenses at relatively high temperatures.

All in all, developing a theory of lunar origins that could make sense of data obtained from the Apollo lunar landing programme proved very difficult. So much so, in fact, that when I took a class on our planetary system from Irwin Shapiro two decades ago, he joked that the best explanation was observational error—the Moon does not exist.

Around that time a new theory was proposed, one which relied on a giant off-centre impact by an exceptionally large planetesimal to eject material from Earth's mantle into terrestrial orbit, from which it could have grown into the Moon.[4, 5] Such an impact would generate a massive cloud of silicate vapour, which could provide the forces needed to place much of the ejecta into stable orbits about the Earth. This model appeared to satisfy the basic dynamical and chemical constraints of the problem, and it won widespread acceptance at the "Origin of the Moon" conference in 1984.[6]

Subsequent modeling of the impact supported the basic scheme of events (although it now seems that gravitational torques were more important than gas pressure in preventing the impact ejecta from falling back to Earth in less than one orbit, and that the mantle of the impactor contributed a substantial fraction of the mass ending up in terrestrial orbit). Modelling also revealed that the impactor would need to be at least comparable in mass to the planet Mars,[7,8] that is, about one-tenth as massive as the Earth.

Only recently, however, has the process of lunar accretion in such an impact-generated disk been simulated in any detail, which is where a paper by Ida, Canup and Stewart[9] comes in. This is by far the most detailed simulation of lunar growth in an impact-generated disk published to date. Ida *et al.* use direct N-body simulations to show that a single dominant moon is usually able to grow from such a disk. However, most of the disk material orbiting near or interior to Roche's tidal limit of accretion at the beginning of the simulation is lost to the planet. (Tidal forces increase rapidly as one approaches a planet; these tides can be strong enough to rip a body apart, and Roche's tidal limit is the location inside which a satellite held together only by its self-gravity will be torn apart by the tidal force of its primary.) The implication here is that lunar growth in an impact-produced disk is not very efficient. So, to form our Moon, more material must be placed in orbit at a greater distance from Earth than was previously believed.

Simulations by Cameron[8] . . . dealt with protolunar disk formation. If both his results and those of Ida *et al.*

prove correct, they suggest that the impactor needed to form a disk large and massive enough to create the Moon would have had to have been more than twice as massive as Mars, and that it must have provided the Earth-Moon system with a few times as much angular momentum as the system currently possesses. This presents two difficulties.

First, how was this "excess" angular momentum lost (solar tides have removed a small amount, but far less than required)? If the Earth was rapidly rotating before the impact, this problem might be less severe, but such simulations have not yet been performed. Second, simulations of the late stages of terrestrial-planet growth[10] imply that an Earth-sized planet is fairly likely to accrete a body roughly as massive as Mars during its growth, so a substantially offcentre impact of a body this size could occur during the growth of tens of per cent of Earth-like bodies, and Moon-like companions to Earth-like planets might be fairly common. But if a much more massive impactor is required, then the Earth-Moon system may be something of an anomaly. The only extrasolar terrestrial planets thus far discovered orbit pulsars, but according to theory there are billions of such planets in our Galaxy. If the new simulations are correct, most of these planets do not have Moon-sized satellites unless they form by some mechanism other than a giant impact.

References

1. Darwin, G. H. *Phil. Trans. R. Soc. II* **170**, 447–538 (1879).
2. Boss, A. P. & Peale, S. J. in *Origin of the Moon* (eds. Hartmann, W. K., Phillips, R. J. & Taylor, G. J.) 59–101 (Lunar & Planetary Institute, Houston, TX, 1986).
3. Ruskol, E. L. *The Moon* **6**, 190–201 (1973).
4. Hartmann, W. K. & Davis, D. R. *Icarus* **24**, 504–515 (1975).

5. Cameron, A. G. W. & Ward, W. R. *Lunar Sci.* **VII**, 120–122 (1976).
6. Hartmann, W. K., Phillips, R. J. & Taylor, G. J. (eds.) *Origin of the Moon* (Lunar & Planetary Institute, Houston, TX, 1986).
7. Benz, W., Slattery, W. L. & Cameron, A. G. W. *Icarus* **71**, 30–45 (1987).
8. Cameron, A. G. W. *Icarus* **126**, 126–137 (1997).
9. Ida, S., Canup, R. M. & Stewart, G. R. *Nature* **389**, 353–357 (1997).
10. Wetherill, G. W. *Science* **228**, 877-879 (1985).

Almost all of the moons and planets in the solar system complete one rotation within a matter of hours. Earth and Mars both spin once in approximately twenty-four hours. Jupiter and Saturn take slightly more than ten hours to complete one rotation. So it came as a big surprise when astronomers discovered a planetary-sized body far beyond Pluto, called Sedna, that takes only forty days to complete one rotation. The object is only 800–1,100 miles (1,287–1,770 km) in diameter and should be rotating much faster compared to similar-size bodies in the solar system.

The best explanation for Sedna's slow rotation is that it has an unseen moon whose gravitational pull is slowing its rotation. The moon's gravity would rob momentum from the spinning body, thus conserving the energy and momentum of the planet-moon system.

Following detailed observations made by the Hubble Space Telescope, astronomers were

*surprised when they didn't find the suspected
moon. If, in fact, there is a moon, it's too dark for
astronomers to see, or it was pulled away from
Sedna by an encounter with another celestial
object. Another alternative is that there is no
moon at all, making Sedna's slow rotation
even more mysterious. Using the principle of
the conservation of energy and momentum, the
author of the following article attempts to solve
the mystery of why Sedna spins so slowly. —RV*

"The Missing Moon of Sedna"
by NASA staff
NASA.gov, April 14, 2004

Astronomers studying thirty-five Hubble Space
Telescope (HST) images of the solar system's farthest
known object, unofficially named Sedna, are surprised
that it does not appear to have a companion moon of
any substantial size. This unexpected result might offer
new clues to the origin and evolution of objects on the
far edge of the solar system.

Sedna's existence was announced on March 15. Its
discoverer, Mike Brown of the California Institute of
Technology, Pasadena, Calif., was so convinced it had a
satellite, that an artist's concept of Sedna released to the
media included a hypothetical moon.

Brown's prediction of a moon is based on Sedna's
slow rotation: it appears to turn on its axis once every
40 days. For comparison, almost all solitary bodies in
the solar system like comets and asteroids rotate once

in a matter of hours. Sedna's more leisurely spin could best be explained, reasoned Brown and colleagues, by the gravitational tug of a companion object acting to slow Sedna's rotation.

"I'm completely baffled at the absence of a moon," Brown said. "This is outside the realm of expectation and makes Sedna even more interesting. But I simply don't know what it means."

Immediately following the announcement of the discovery of Sedna, NASA astronomers turned the HST toward the new planetoid to search for the expected companion. The space-based platform provides the resolving power needed to make such precision measurements. "Sedna's image isn't stable enough in ground-based telescopes," Brown said.

Surprisingly, the HST images, taken March 16 with the new Advanced Camera for Surveys, only show the single object Sedna, along with a faint, very distant background star in the same field of view.

Even with Hubble's crisp view, it may just be barely resolving the disk of Sedna, Brown said. It's equivalent to trying to see a soccer ball 900 miles away. The Hubble images place an upper limit on Sedna's diameter of approximately three-quarters the size of Pluto, or about 1,000 miles across.

Brown had expected the moon to pop up as a companion "dot" in Hubble's images, but the object is simply not there. There is a chance it might have been behind Sedna or transiting in front of it, so it could not be seen separately from Sedna in the HST images. But the chance of that is very low.

Brown's estimate of Sedna's 40-day rotation period comes from observations of apparent periodic changes in light reflecting from Sedna's mottled surface. Sedna appears to be the slowest rotating object in the solar system after Mercury and Venus, whose slow rotation rates are due to the tidal influence of the sun. One easy way out of this dilemma is the possibility the rotation period is not as slow as astronomers thought. But even with a careful reanalysis, the team remains convinced the period is correct.

Brown admits, "I'm completely lost for an explanation as to why the object rotates so slowly."

Courtesy of NASA.

Assuming that Earth's moon was made from debris that was thrown off the planet during a collision with another body, there still exists the question of exactly how that debris came to form our moon. Computer simulations show that much of the impacting body was assimilated into Earth, but some debris was tossed into a ring around Earth, much like the ring of Saturn.

Under a variety of fast-acting forces and dynamics, objects from that ring wound up coming together into what we now know as the Moon in just about a month. The impact converted kinetic energy to heat. The debris from the impact was flung away from Earth and carried

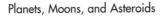

some of Earth's rotational energy—angular momentum—with it. The debris with the highest angular momentum settled into a disk in which dust and rocks began coming together.

The inner part of the ring rotated faster than the outer part of the ring. This motion caused the disk to form spiral arms. The spiral arms fed material out beyond the tips of the arms, where it quickly came to form our moon.

In "Evolution of a Circumterrestrial Disk and Formation of a Single Moon," Eiichiro Kokubo and coauthors analyze several different models of how our moon may have formed following the principle of conservation of energy and momentum. —RV

From "Evolution of a Circumterrestrial Disk and Formation of a Single Moon"
by Eiichiro Kokubo, Shigeru Ida, and Junichiro Makino
Icarus, March 9, 2000

We investigate the evolution of a circumterrestrial disk of debris generated by a giant impact on Earth and the dynamical characteristics of the moon accreted from the disk. We find that in most cases the disk evolution results in the formation of a single large moon on a nearly circular orbit close to the equatorial plane of the initial disk just outside the Roche limit . . . The efficiency of incorporation of disk material into a moon is 10–55 %, which increases with the initial specific angular momentum of the disk. These results hardly depend on the initial condition of the disk as long as the mass of the disk is 2 to 4 times the present lunar mass and most mass of the disk exists inside the Roche limit.

The timescale of the disk evolution is determined mainly by the surface density of the disk because mass transfer to the outside of the Roche limit and formation of lunar seeds are regulated by collective behavior of disk particles. The evolution of the disk is summarized as follows: The disk contracts through collisional damping. As the velocity dispersion of disk particles decreases, particle clumps grow inside the Roche limit. The clumps become elongated due to Keplerian shear, which forms spiral arm-like structure. Particles are transferred to the outside of the Roche limit through the gravitational torque exerted by the spiral arms. When a tip of a spiral arm goes beyond the Roche limit, it collapses into a small moonlet. The rapid accretion of these small moonlets forms a lunar seed. The seed exclusively grows by sweeping up particles transfered over the Roche limit. When the moon becomes large enough to gravitationally dominate the disk, it pushes the rest of the inner disk to Earth. The formation timescale of the moon is of the order of 1 month if a particulate disk is assumed and the effect of melting/vaporization is not included.

Introduction

In the "giant impact" scenario, the Moon is accreted from a circumterrestrial disk of debris generated by the impact of a Mars-sized protoplanet with early Earth (Hartman and Davis 1975, Cameron and Ward 1976).

This model has been favored as it can potentially account for major dynamical and geochemical characteristics of the present Earth–Moon system: the system's high angular momentum and depletion of volatiles and iron in the lunar material (e.g., Stevenson 1987). On the other hand, the recent studies of planetary formation revealed that in the late stage of planetary accretion, protoplanets are formed through runaway growth of planetesimals (e.g., Greenberg *et al.* 1978, Wetherill and Stewart 1989, Weidenschilling *et al.* 1997, Kokubo and Ida 1998). In the final stage of the terrestrial planet formation, collisions among protoplanets with sweeping up of residual planetesimals would be likely (e.g., Lissauer and Stewart 1993). Thus, giant impacts may be plausible events.

Giant impacts have been modeled by using a smoothed-particle hydrodynamics (SPH) (Benz *et al.* 1986, 1987, 1989. Cameron and Benz 1991, Cameron 1997). The impacts between two protoplanets with iron cores and silicate mantles were calculated. It is found that an impact by a Mars-sized protoplanet usually results in formation of a circumterrestrial debris disk. The initial disk may possibly be a hot silicate vapor atmosphere. In this case, as the disk cools down, it condenses into many small solid particles. In most cases, a significant amount of the disk material exists within the Roche limit, where the tidal force of Earth inhibits gravitational binding of lunar material.

The accretion process of the moon from the impact-generated disk was first investigated by Canup and Esposito (1996). They showed that in general many small moonlets are formed initially rather than a single large moon. However, it is difficult to include global effects such as radial migration of lunar material and interaction of formed moons with the disk and collective effects such as the formation of particle aggregates and spiral arms in the gas model. These effects are potentially very important in the evolution of the disk.

Ida *et al.* (1997) (hereafter 1CS97) performed the first N-body simulation of lunar accretion from the circumterrestrial disk. In N-body simulation, global and collective effects are automatically taken into account. They showed that the typical outcome of the accretion from the disk is the formation of a single large moon as long as most disk mass is initially within the Roche limit. Their calculations also establish a direct relationship between the size of the accreted moon and the initial configuration of the circumterrestrial disk.

In the present paper, we present high-resolution N-body calculation of the lunar accretion from a circumterrestrial disk of debris generated by a giant impact on Earth. Since accretion of large bodies from circumplanetary disks may be a common phenomenon in planetary systems, it is important to clarify basic dynamics in the evolution of circumplanetary disks.

Inside the Roche limit particle clumps develop as the velocity dispersion of disk particles decreases and are sheared to form spiral arms. The lunar material is transfered beyond the Roche limit through the gravitational torque exerted by the spiral arms. The collapse of material into moonlets outside the Roche limit and their subsequent pairwise accretion form a lunar seed.

In most cases, a single large moon is formed on a nearly noninclined circular orbit just outside the Roche limit. This result hardly depends on the initial condition of the disk as long as the disk mass is a few times the present lunar mass and the disk is compact; in other words, most mass of the disk exists inside the Roche limit. The timescale of the lunar accretion is of the order of 1 month as long as a particulate disk is considered. We show that not the mass of individual particles but the surface density of the disk mainly controls the key processes of moon formation such as mass transfer over the Roche limit and subsequent formation of moonlets. The final mass of the moon is determined by the conservation of mass and angular momentum of the initial disk . . .

Accretion Model

We adopt three types of accretion models. In the present paper, "accretion" means merging two particles into one spherical particle. In principle, we do not take into account collisional fragmentation of particles. The inclusion of fragmentation may not affect accretion of a large moon, . . . although detailed study of its effect should be done in the future work . . .

In accretion, orbital angular momentum of colliding particles is not exactly conserved since a part of the orbital angular momentum is transfered to the spin angular momentum that is neglected in our calculation. However, this spin angular momentum is much smaller than the orbital angular momentum . . . Thus, in accretion, angular momentum is almost conserved . . .

The mass of the largest bound aggregate gradually decreases due to collisions and tidal stripping. The effective density of an aggregate is usually smaller than the lunar material since constituent particles of the aggregate are not filled up most tightly. The reduction of the effective density is the highest in the equal mass particle case. With a size distribution of particles, particles can be packed more tightly than the equal-mass particle case. It is easier for particles to escape from the gravitational field of the aggregate with lower density. However, in the realistic lunar accretion, particles would melt partially or totally at collisions and then the density of an aggregate (moonlet) would be as large as the lunar material. The lower effective density also enhances the collisional cross section. In these points, the two accretion models are preferable.

In the total and partial accretion models, there is sometimes a relatively large moonlet inside the Roche limit as a result of gravitational scattering. In the rubble pile model, there are no stable aggregates inside the Roche limit due to strong Keplerian shear . . . Thus, the moonlet inside the Roche limit would not be realistic. It must be destroyed by the shear. In this point, the rubble pile model is better.

In principle, the results of the total and partial accretion models and the rubble pile model are similar quantitatively over relatively short dynamical timescales. Over long dynamical time-scales, the rubble pile model slightly differs because in the rubble pile model, the moon (aggregate) loses mass during collisions with other aggregates and through tidal stripping. The results of both total and partial accretion models are essentially the same over long dynamical timescales. In order to survey dynamical characteristics of the moon accreted from disks with various initial conditions, we use the total and partial accretion models to avoid the unrealistic decrease of the lunar mass and the high calculation cost of the rubble pile model. We adopt the rubble pile model to see the evolution of the spatial structure of the disk in the initial stage, since it is clearer in the rubble pile model than in the two accretion models.

Results

We investigated the evolution of a circumterrestrial disk with 30 different initial conditions using three accretion models. The disk evolution is qualitatively similar for all the runs though the initial condition of the disk and the accretion model are different in each run. We investigated the initial stage of the evolution of the circumterrestrial disk mainly by the rubble pile model . . . In most cases, a single large moon is formed on a nearly circular orbit close to the equatorial plane of the initial disk just outside the Roche limit. This result hardly depends on the initial conditions of the disk and the accretion model we adopted . . .

Disk Evolution

The evolution of the disk is divided into two stages namely, the rapid growth and the slow growth stages . . . The duration of the rapid growth stage . . . is about 1 month. The formation of the moon is almost completed in this stage. The slow growth stage . . . is the cleaning up stage where the moon sweeps up or scatters away the residual disk particles. The growth rate in this stage is very low.

In the rapid growth stage, the redistribution of disk mass through angular momentum transfer supplies material for accretion outside of the Roche limit: most of the disk mass falls to Earth while some of the mass is transported outward . . .

Mass transfer by the spiral arms. Particles are transfered to the outside of the Roche limit through the gravitational torque exerted by the spiral arms, in compensation for falling down of many particles to Earth. The surface density inside the Roche limit decreases with time because of the mass transfer to Earth and to the outside of the Roche limit. On the other hand, the surface density outside the Roche limit increases through the supply of material from the inside of the Roche limit . . .

Collapse of aggregates. When a tip of a spiral arm goes beyond the Roche limit, it collapses into a small aggregate . . . (the formation of bound aggregates in the rubble pile model corresponds to the formation of moonlets in the partial and total accretion models) . . .

Growth of the lunar seed. After the formation of the lunar seed, it stays just outside the Roche limit and exclusively grows by sweeping up particles transfered beyond the Roche limit. As the lunar seed grows, it moves gradually outward due to interaction with the inner disk . . . As the moon is primarily formed by the material transfered beyond the Roche limit, the timescale of the moon formation is almost equivalent to the timescale of the mass transfer due to the gravitational torque by spiral arms. The timescale of mass transfer is also almost equivalent to that of angular momentum transfer in the disk . . . The timescale of moon formation depends on not the individual mass of disk particles but the surface density of the disk. Ward and Cameron (1977) obtained almost the same timescale by considering the energy dissipation in the clumps formed by gravitational instability.

The spiral structure is not always clear in the disk since it is often destroyed by gravitational scattering by large moonlets. However, the mass transfer rate hardly changes. This is because for the mass transfer, the important point is not only a spiral structure but also a nonaxisymmetric structure. Detailed investigation of the angular momentum transfer in a circumterrestrial disk by Takeda and Ida (2000 in progress) showed that angular momentum transfered by nonaxisymmetric clumps is always as large as that due to gravitational torque exerted by the spirals. They also showed that the angular momentum transfer by these collective processes is the main driver for angular momentum transfer near the Roche limit as long as the initial number of disk particles is larger than a few thousands for the disks concerned here . . . The result of the rubble pile model showed that the lunar seed is formed by not gradual pairwise accretion of disk particles but collective particle processes: formation of clumps by gravitational instability, angular momentum transfer due to the gravitational torque by the spiral arms, and collapse and collision of particle aggregates. The size of clumps and the radial wavelength of spiral arms are determined by the critical wavelength of the disk, which is the function of the surface density. Mass transfer is driven by the gravitational torque by the spiral arms, whose timescale depends on the surface density. Overall, it is the surface density of the disk, rather than the properties of the individual particles, that governs the evolution of the disk . . .

Summary and Discussion

. . . The evolution of the above disks results in formation of a single large moon on a nearly circular orbit close to the equatorial plane of the initial disk just outside the Roche limit.

The evolution of the circumterrestrial disk is summarized as follows:

1. The disk contracts through collisional damping of particles.

2. Particle clumps grow inside the Roche limit as the velocity dispersion of particles decreases.

3. The clumps are elongated by Keplerian shear, which forms spiral arms. The spiral arms are smoothed out as they wind up and then the formation of spiral arms is repeated.

4. Particles are transfered to outside of the Roche limit through the gravitational torque exerted by the spiral arms.

5. When a tip of the spiral arm goes beyond the Roche limit, it collapses to form a small

moonlet. The rapid accretion of these small moonlets forms a lunar seed.

6. The seed exclusively grows by sweeping up particles transfered beyond the Roche limit.

7. When the moon becomes large enough to gravitationally dominate the disk, it pushes the rest of the inner disk to Earth.

The moon is almost completed by the stage 5 . . . This timescale hardly depends on the detailed initial conditions of the disk we simulated since the timescales of important processes in lunar formation such as mass transfer is regulated mainly by the surface density of the disk. The reason why a single large moon is the outcome of the disk evolution is now clear. As the disk evolves as described above, the formation of a single large moon seems an inevitable outcome . . .

Most planets in the Solar System have satellites, which suggests that satellites are natural by-products of planet formation. In addition, there are various satellite systems from a single large moon to small multiple moons with-rings. In the standard scenario of satellite formation, most of them are believed to be formed from circumplanetary disks. In the present paper, we focused on the moon formation from an impact-generated disk. We can extend the framework of the moon formation to various satellite systems. An example is the Pluto–Charon system. Charon has the largest mass ratio to the central planet (Pluto) of about 1/7 in the Solar System. The giant impact scenario is a strong candidate for its origin. If we consider a more massive disk than the present moon case, a very massive satellite may form from the disk.

Another example is the multiple satellite system like the saturnian system. If the initial disk is less massive and radially well extended over the Roche limit, accretion is possible well outside the Roche limit, which may result in a multiple moon system with a disk inside the Roche limit. After all, the diversity of satellite systems may mainly come from the initial condition of the circumplanetary disk such as mass and angular momentum.

References

Benz, W., A. G. W. Cameron, and H. J. Melosh 1989. The origin of the Moon and the single impact hypothesis. III. *Icarus* **81**, 113–131.

Benz, W., W. L. Slattery, and A. G. W. Cameron 1986. The origin of the Moon and the single impact hypothesis. I. *Icarus* **66**, 515–535.

Benz, W., W. L. Slattery, and A. G. W. Cameron 1987. The origin of the Moon and the single impact hypothesis. II. *Icarus* **71**, 30–45.

Cameron, A. G. W. 1997. The origin of the Moon and the single impact hypothesis. V. *Icarus* **126**, 126–137.

Cameron, A. G. W., and W. Benz 1991. The origin of the Moon and the single impact hypothesis. IV. *Icarus* **92**, 204–216.

Cameron, A. G. W., and W. R. Ward 1976. The origin of the Moon. *Proc. Lunar Planet. Sci. Confi 7th*, 120–122.

Cameron, A. G. W., and R. M. Canup 1998a. The giant impact occurred during Earth accretion. *Proc. Lunar Planet. Sci. Conf 29th*.

Cameron, A. G. W., and R. M. Canup 1998b. The giant impact and the formation of the Moon. In *Origin of the Earth and Moon*, LPI Contribution 957, 3–4.

Canup, R. M., and L. W. Esposito 1995. Accretion in the Roche zone: Co-existence of rings and ringmoons. *Icarus* **113**, 331–352.

Canup, R. M., and L. W. Esposito 1996. Accretion of the Moon from an impact-generated disk. *Icarus* **119**, 427–446.

Greenberg, R., J. Wacker, C. R. Chapman, and W. K. Hartman 1978. Planetesimals to planets: Numerical simulation of collisional evolution. *Icarus* **35**, 1–26.

Hartmann, W. K., and D. R. Davis 1975. Satellite-sized planetesimals and lunar origin. *Icarus* **24**, 504–515.

Ida, S., R. M. Canup, and O. R. Stewart 1997. Lunar accretion from an impact-generated disk. *Nature* **389**, 353–357.

Kokubo, E., and S. Ida 1998. Oligarchic growth of protoplanets. *Icarus* **131**, 171–178.

Lissauer, J. J., and O. R. Stewart 1993. Growth of planets from planetesimals. In *Protostars and Planets III* (E. H. Levy and J. I. Lunine, Eds.), pp. 1061–1088. Univ. of Arizona Press, Tucson.

Stevenson, D. J. 1987. Origin of the Moon—The collisional hypothesis. *Annu. Rev. Earth Plant. Sci.* **15**, 271–315.

Ward, W. R., and A. G. W. Cameron 1977. Disk evolution within the Roche limit. *Proc. Lunar Planet. Sci. Conf. 9th*, 1205–1207.

The tiny, frigid planetoid Sedna is the largest object detected within our solar system since the discovery of Pluto in 1930. Now a relatively close 8 billion miles (12.9 billion km) from Earth, Sedna wanders out as far as 84 billion miles (135.2 billion km). But where did it come from?

Some scientists suggest that Sedna could have come from a region of comets, called the Kuiper Belt, which stretches from Neptune to just beyond Pluto, and that it had somehow been dislodged and sent off on a more distant orbit.

Another possibility is that Sedna came in from the Oort cloud, a swarm of a trillion comets stretching out to one light-year from the Sun. Sedna could have been separated from the greater cloud by the gravitational pull of a rogue star that came close to the Sun billions of years ago.

When a small body, such as Sedna, passes relatively close to a larger body, such *as a bypassing star, momentum is exchanged and conserved. In this example, Sedna lost orbital energy to the bypassing star and followed a lower-energy orbit that brought it closer to the Sun.*

In "Stray Star May Have Jolted Sedna," Maggie McKee explores the possibilities of how the conservation of energy and momentum could have positioned Sedna in its current place in our solar system. —RV

"Stray Star May Have Jolted Sedna"
by Maggie McKee
New Scientist, July 27, 2004

Sedna, the most distant planetoid ever seen in the Solar System, probably got kicked into its orbit when a star swept past the Sun more than four billion years ago, suggest the first detailed calculations of the object's origins.

The research supports the leading theory of Sedna's origins but also leaves open more outlandish possibilities.

The planetoid, about three-quarters the size of Pluto, was discovered in November 2003. It takes about 12,000 years to traverse an elongated orbit that stretches from 74 to 900 times the distance from the Sun to the Earth. And its journey around the Sun is thought to take Sedna from its present location in the shadowy Kuiper Belt out towards the Oort Cloud at the Solar System's outer edges.

The Kuiper Belt is a mysterious band of rock and ice leftover from the birth of the Solar System, which lies beyond Neptune. The remote Oort Cloud forms a spherical shell of icy bodies around the Solar System and its edges lie many thousands of times Pluto's distance from the Sun.

Sedna's orbit is so extreme researchers say it could not have formed simply from the gravitational kicks of the giant planets, which are responsible for the eccentric orbits of the comets and Pluto.

"If this thing was scattered out by a planet, something else had to change the orbit, something we don't see," says study co-author Hal Levison, an astronomer at the Southwest Research Institute in Boulder, Colorado. "That's why Sedna and 2000 CR 105 [the next most-distant object] are so cool. They tell us something was different back when they formed."

Cluster of Stars

Levison and colleague Alessandro Morbidelli of the Observatoire de la Cote d'Azur in Nice, France, used computer simulations to study five different scenarios for how Sedna and 2000 CR 105 got their orbits.

The most likely scenario supports one of the theories put forward by Sedna's discoverers. They believe the Sun was born in a cluster of stars, and that one or more of those siblings passed by the Sun in the stars' first 100 million years.

The new study recreates Sedna's orbit using this scenario. "I still strongly favour that hypothesis," Sedna's co-discoverer Michael Brown of the California Institute of Technology in Pasadena told *New Scientist*.

But the new study discounts Brown and his colleagues' other main theory—that a planet lying at about 75 times the Sun-Earth distance is responsible for Sedna's orbit. "It's still a possibility, but we haven't found anything there so we don't believe it so much these days," Brown concedes.

Brown Dwarf

The study also quashes other theories, including the hypothesis that Neptune and Uranus, thought to have been in more eccentric orbits in the past, could have pushed Sedna and other bodies outward. Those planets are not massive enough to have done the job in their short eccentric phases, Levison says.

But the researchers thought up another improbable scenario that managed to explain Sedna's orbit remarkably well. Sedna could have been born around a brown dwarf about 20 times less massive than the Sun and captured by our Solar System when the brown dwarf approached.

"What's striking about this idea is how efficient it is," says Levison, whose calculations suggest about half of the material orbiting the dwarf would have gone into orbit around the Sun. "Even if it's wrong it's a cool idea."

"It just seems implausible, but that doesn't mean it's not true," agrees Brown.

Reprinted with permission from *New Scientist*.

There are between 1,050 and 4,200 asteroids of at least 0.6 miles (1 km) in diameter that regularly hurtle across Earth's path. They are called near Earth objects (NEOs).

There are many strategies for changing an asteroid's orbit by accelerating it with additional force. Attaching a nuclear rocket motor to the asteroid could produce the force needed to nudge it. Without carrying propellant to the asteroid and simply using electromagnetic rail gun, we could eject some of the asteroid's material via a mass-driver that continuously slings material off the asteroid. It's like having a giant slingshot powered by magnetism.

By applying Isaac Newton's third law of motion, which states that for every action there is an equal and opposite reaction, the asteroid's velocity and, hence, trajectory would change. It is analogous to standing on a sled on ice and throwing bricks off the sled. The sled will begin to move in the opposite direction from the trajectory of the bricks. In terms of changing the asteroid's orbit, the recoil would nudge the asteroid onto a different course. It's not too early to try one of these strategies on a test asteroid, one that has no chance of ever coming close to Earth should the experiment fail. —RV

From "Deflecting NEOs in Route of Collision with the Earth"
by Andrea Carusi, Giovanni B. Valsecchi,
Germano D'Abramo, and Andrea Boattini
Icarus, March 7, 2002

The problem of deflecting near Earth objects (NEOs) in course of collision with the Earth has been extensively studied during the past decade within the planetological community and a chapter of the well-known book *Hazards Due to Comets and Asteroids* (Gehrels 1994) was entirely devoted to this subject.

In the existing literature both the orbit perturbation requirements (impulsive velocity change, Δv, required to deflect Earth-impacting trajectories) and several physical means for deflecting or explosively fragmenting asteroids and comets were preliminarily examined. Ahrens and Harris (1992, 1994) gave an analytical order-of-magnitude estimate of impulsive Δv based on the two-body circular orbit approximation (Sun-asteroid). They showed that the most effective way to deflect an orbiting body is to apply Δv along the track of motion.

Ahrens and Harris (1992, 1994) also presented some viable strategies, according to the technology lore of the epoch, for diverting asteroids and comets such as direct-impact deflection, mass drivers, deflection by nuclear explosion radiation, or surface nuclear explosive, and they analyzed them under the orbit perturbation requirements. They also explored the secureness and the efficiency of nuclear fragmentation and dispersal.

Moreover, Willoughby *et al.* (1994) studied the feasibility of using nuclear thermal propulsion systems, namely nuclear thermal engines, while Melosh *et al.* (1994) explored more specifically nonnuclear means of deflecting threatening objects; the most exotic means were solar sails, solar radiation collectors, and laser systems.

From these studies some preliminary conclusions may be drawn. First of all that deflection methods seem to be preferable to fragmentation approaches because the latter require more energy and are less secure. Moreover, among the deflecting methods it seems that for asteroids less than 100 m wide the most practical method is kinetic energy impact, while for objects in the 1–10 km range deflection by nuclear explosive radiation seems to be the simplest approach.

However, the use of very large (Gigaton) weapons undoubtedly raises some perplexities. While it is believed that this kind of approach requires less detailed knowledge of the physical characteristics of the Earth-crossing objects, we think that probably the opposite is true. In fact, the behavior of the asteroid or comet under the stress wave induced by the stand-off nuclear blast cannot be known a priori, unless a detailed study of the mineralogical and mechanical characteristics is carried out in situ, through space probes. And that inevitably weakens one of the main advantages of this kind of deflection procedure, that is, its capability to be set up in a rather short time, as required when the advance time before impact is too small for other approaches.

Moreover, we would have practically no control on the effects of such an "energetic" approach if something goes wrong, not to mention the risk inherent in the mere existence of an arsenal of such high potential weapons and about the risk of failure in orbiting them . . .

In this paper we will not deal with the technical and engineering aspects involved in planning a true deflection procedure, including the study of possible mission profiles for testing deflection methods; actually, the aim of the present work is to give a numerical verification of the above-mentioned orbit perturbation requirements. We selected a suitable sample of existing NEOs (the criterion for the choice is explained in the following section) and slightly modified their orbits in order to make them Earth impactors. For each of these colliding trajectories we explored, by means of a full N-body numerical orbit integrator, the modulus of the impulsive along-track Δv required to avoid a collision, as a function of the time before impact. In our analysis we do not include interior physical properties of the asteroids and comets, such as internal stresses and rotation: we treat them as geometrical points with mass.

We note that when the orbit of the colliding NEO is such that it does not experience close encounters with the Earth before the epoch of the impact, the analytical approximation of Δv given by Ahrens and Harris (1992, 1994) is in acceptable good agreement with the numerical results. On the other hand, when the colliding object has some pre-impact close encounters with the Earth, namely when the two-body approximation used by Ahrens and Harris (1992, 1994) fails, we spot some interesting features. For instance, in some cases these close encounters facilitate the deflection, lowering the magnitude of the required Δv.

To the authors' knowledge, the present study is the first published paper on a systematic numerical analysis of the variation of Δv with respect to the impact advance time. Moreover, in this work we give a comparison between our numerical results and the results obtained through a new analytical theory of planetary encounters (Valsecchi *et al.* 2001).

Objective and Computational Details

To gain insight into the problems related to deflection of incoming objects on an impact course with the Earth, we have performed a number of simulations involving bodies (both asteroids and comets) on orbits with different dynamical characteristics. As a matter of fact, the primary purpose of these simulations was to relate the variation of the heliocentric velocity Δv, necessary to make the object miss the Earth, to the time at which the maneuver is applied, in a number of different dynamical situations.

Defining the "epoch of interception" as the time lapse between a maneuver aimed at deflecting an incoming object and the time of the anticipated impact, our problem translates into three basic questions:

- What is the Δv necessary to avoid an impact, as a function of the epoch of interception?
- How does the effect of a suitable maneuver depend on the object's orbital characteristics?

- Can we identify in advance the best opportunities and predict the outcome of a maneuver?

To answer these questions we have chosen 11 objects, mostly on the basis of the small values of their minimum orbital intersection distance (MOID) or of their intrinsic interest as representatives of specific dynamical types of NEOs. These objects are: the short-period comets IP/Halley, 73P/Schwassmann–Wachmann 3, and 109P/Swift–Tuttle; the asteroids Hermes, 1996 JA_1, 1997 XF_{11}, 1998 WT_{24}, 1999 AN_{10}, 1999 AQ_{10}, and 2000 EH_{26}; and the transitional object (4015) Wilson—Harrington. All the source orbits have been taken from the MPC catalogues. The first step in the procedure has then been to "force" an impact between the object and the Earth at a suitable epoch. To do this it has been necessary to modify the original orbits, in some cases by large amounts. The resulting orbits, therefore, do not represent the "real" objects, but fictitious cases that are similar to the real objects. The modified orbits have then been integrated backward in time to an epoch preceding the impact by 50 years: integrating forward from this point, all objects impacted the Earth after 50 years.

The dynamical model used in all integrations was quite simplified: it included the Sun, the Earth, and the Moon separately, Mars, Jupiter, and Saturn . . . Once the start orbits have been obtained, the subsequent procedure included three more steps:

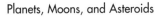

1. integrate forward up to the impact, recording time, position, and velocity of the object at each integration step,

2. restart from each integration step applying a slight Δv along track (i.e., along the instantaneous velocity vector line) in both the positive and negative directions,

3. iterate the above step until a Δv value is found for which the impact turns into a grazing encounter. Record the Δv value needed to achieve this result.

At the end of this process we got two files for each object: one with the positive Δv values needed to miss the Earth and one with the negative values. These values were then plotted as a function of time . . .

Concluding Remarks

We have presented in this paper some numerical simulations of deflection of incoming bodies. We have seen that the Δv values to be imparted to the object in order to avoid the impact depend largely on the epoch of interception and on the orbital properties of the objects.

In some cases, when close encounters with the Earth are rather rare, the needed Δv changes quite smoothly over decades, rising by an order of magnitude in almost 40 years. In such cases the time at which the maneuver is applied would not be extremely critical, but certainly an early maneuver would be preferable . . . In addition, it would be extremely important to understand clearly the geometry of the impact. If the impact is not central the effect of a deflecting maneuver applied in the two possible, opposite directions may differ considerably.

In other cases, when pre-impact encounters are present close to the impact epoch, it would be important to apply the maneuver before the last pre-impact encounter, in order to take advantage of the amplification to which such a maneuver would be subject. This is especially true for those objects which exhibit "resonant returns," because in these cases the epoch of interception may be rather close to the impact epoch. We have also shown that it is possible to analytically compute the effect of a deflecting maneuver with a good approximation, at least for cases in which the orbit of the object is not too close to strong resonances with the Earth.

However, this work does not take into account all the problems related to the *mechanics* of such maneuvers. In a real case it would be fundamental to have a very good knowledge of physical and mechanical parameters of the object to be deflected, such as the rotation state, the surface characteristics and internal strength, the location of the center of mass, the strength and properties of "bridges" between contact binaries, etc.

The knowledge of these parameters is always necessary, but for some of them it acquires a particular relevance depending on the deflection technique used. It is the intention of the authors to start modeling more realistic cases in the near future in the framework of a study for the Italian Space Agency (Carusi 2001).

References

Ahrens, T. J., and A. W. Harris 1992. Deflection and fragmentation of near-Earth asteroids. *Nature* **360**, 429–433.

Ahrens, T. J., and A. W. Harris 1994. Deflection and fragmentation of near-Earth asteroids. In *Hazards Due to Comets and Asteroids* (T. Gehrels, Ed.), pp. 897–927. Univ. of Arizona Press, Tucson.

Carusi, A. (Coordinator) 2001. Applicabilitiy del propulsore 242 al problema della deflessione di asteroidi in rotta di collisione con Ia Terra. Approved research project, ASI, Rome. [In Italian]

Gehrels, T. (Ed.) 1994. *Hazards Due to Comets and Asteroids.* Univ. of Arizona Press, Tucson.

Melosh, H. J., I. V. Nemchinov, and Yu. I. Zetzer 1994. Non-nuclear strategies for deflecting comets and asteroids. In *Hazards Due to Comets and Asteroids* (T. Gehrels, Ed.), pp. 1111–1132. Univ. of Arizona Press, Tucson.

Valsecchi, G. B., A. Milani, G. F. Gronchi, and S. R. Chesley 2001. Resonant return to close approach: Analytical theory. Astron. Astrophys., submitted.

Willoughby A. J., M. L. McGuire, S. K. Borowski, and S. D. Howe 1994. The role of nuclear thermal propulsion in mitigating Earth-threatening asteroids. In *Hazards Due to Comets and Asteroids* (T. Gehrels, Ed.). Univ. of Arizona Press, Tucson.

Reprinted from *Icarus*, Vol. 159, by Andrea Carusi, Giovanni B. Valsecchi, Germano D'Abramo, and Andrea Boattini, "Deflecting NEOs in route of collision with the Earth," pp. 417–422, © 2002, with permission from Elsevier.

4 Energy in the Universe

Sound carries energy in the form of waves. Just imagine a clap of thunder from a lightning bolt. The longer the distance between successive peaks of waves, like the ripples made by a stone tossed into a pond, the longer the wavelength and the lower the pitch.

In "Songs of the Galaxies, and What They Mean," Dennis Overbye looks at a deep cosmic bass produced by energy from a black hole. The energy waves spread out as ripples from the cavity of the black hole. Jets of material push through gas surrounding the black hole. The jets move through space with tremendous momentum, traveling near the speed of light.

The energy from these jets is converted to energy waves, which spread out in all directions and keep the gas near the galaxy warm. This prevents the cluster from cooling, collapsing, and turning into stars. Considering this, conservation of energy, in this situation, is a major factor in the evolution of the universe. —RV

"Songs of the Galaxies, and What They Mean"
by Dennis Overbye
New York Times, August 3, 2004

Another black hole is singing, although it seems a little tone-deaf.

Last year, astronomers discovered that outbursts from a giant black hole were spreading pressure waves through the thin hot gas of the distant Perseus cluster of galaxies. The frequency of these waves was equivalent to a B flat, 57 octaves below middle C, the astronomers calculated.

Now another group of astronomers has discovered waves from another massive black hole spreading outward from the center of a galaxy known as M87 at the heart of the Virgo cluster, about 50 million light-years from Earth. They appear as rings and arcs of brightness in images of the galaxy obtained by NASA's Chandra X-Ray Observatory.

The sound waves in M87, spaced about four million years apart, are a little more than an octave higher than the Perseus black hole, they said, and a little rougher and less pure.

"If one could hear the sound, it would be more like the cannons in the '1812 Overture' than the pure tone of a musical instrument," said Dr. William Forman of the Harvard-Smithsonian Center for Astrophysics.

Frivolous as it may sound, the phenomenon is part of a changing picture of the relation between galaxies (and the other luminous structures that web the sky) and black holes, the Einsteinian monsters that seem to dwell in the heart of almost every galaxy.

In this view, black holes may regulate both their own growth and the growth of their galaxies by explosive outbursts, orchestrating the flow of gas that is essential to the formation of stars, the lifeblood of the luminous universe.

Dr. Abraham Loeb, a theorist at the Harvard-Smithsonian Center, said, "People have only recently come to realize that the central black holes affect the formation of galaxies in a profound way."

Because it is nearly next door in cosmic terms, M87 is a natural laboratory for examining how black holes relate to the galaxies around them.

"Now we see how the black hole grows, how it affects the gas from which it grows," Dr. Forman said. "It all seems to connect."

Dr. Forman is part of a multinational team of astronomers that has used Chandra and other X-ray satellites to study what is going on in M87, and the lead author of a paper submitted to *The Astrophysical Journal*.

Speaking of the Virgo and Perseus results, Dr. Christine Jones of the Harvard-Smithsonian Center, also on the team, said, "We are seeing evidence of recurrent outbursts of the black holes in these galaxies."

It may seem contradictory to talk about a black hole releasing energy. According to Einstein's general theory of relativity, black holes are so dense that neither matter nor energy nor light nor anything else, including sound, can escape from them. They are sheer gravitational death.

Nothing but inexorable doom, crushing and stretching, awaits anything that enters. A famous calculation by the Cambridge University theorist Dr. Stephen Hawking 30 years ago showed that when quantum effects are taken into account, black holes would leak and eventually explode, but the process would take much longer than the age of the universe, and so is little comfort.

But black holes can produce energy in the space around them by virtue of their enormous gravitational fields. Long before any infalling material, whether astronaut or gas cloud, reached the point of no return, it would be accelerated to nearly the speed of light and heated to millions of degrees, sparking X-rays and high-energy particles, as it swirled in a thick dense disk around the cosmic drain.

As a result of enormous pressure and magnetic fields, some of that stuff would never make it into the hole but would be squeezed like toothpaste and shot across space, away from the black hole in two oppositely directed jets.

The more black holes eat, the more they spill, and it is widely thought that their feeding frenzies power the violence seen in the nuclei of many galaxies, including the powerful quasars that are so bright they outshine their parent galaxies. Although the most massive black holes amount to only a tiny fraction of the mass of their galaxies, a tenth of a percent at most, they release huge quantities of energy, Dr. Loeb pointed out.

A wealth of observations of M87 over the years have illuminated, in messy, chaotic detail, the feeding habits of its central black hole, estimated to weigh in at two billion to three billion times the mass of the Sun. Dr. Forman said evidence of the messiness includes a sharp knotted spike, or jet, of energetic particles shooting from the galaxy's core; giant lobes of radio energy extending far out into intergalactic space; other bubbles and cavities, apparently inflated by the jet, in the inner regions of the galaxy; and a pair of arms of X-ray emission, one of which resembles the column of a rising mushroom cloud from a nuclear explosion.

The jet and an invisible counterpart going in the opposite direction, crashing into interstellar gas, seem to create the galaxy's discordant drum roll. In the new work, Dr. Forman and his collaborators combined two different Chandra pictures and data from the German Rosat and the European Space Agency's XMM-Newton satellites. The sound waves appear as bright arcs in the X-ray glow of hot gas that suffuses the M87 galaxy and the Virgo cluster in which it sits.

One of them makes an entire circle around the nucleus, at a radius of about 45,000 light-years. Another arc sits at a radius of about 57,000 light-years from the center. The most recent outburst, they estimated, was about 11 million years ago and was the equivalent of about 10 million supernova explosions.

The results echo the earlier ones from the Perseus cluster and strengthen the conclusion that through their outbursts black holes may be reaching across intergalactic space and controlling the fates of billions of stars not yet born.

Clusters of galaxies are the largest assemblages of matter in the universe, with masses up to a trillion Suns.

Most of the ordinary matter in them, however, is not in the form of stars but in a dilute gas that has been heated to millions of degrees by falling into the cluster. It has long been a puzzle why this gas does not cool off, fall into the center of the cluster and make new stars.

Now it seems that singing black holes are heating the gas and keeping it from falling.

"This certainly shows that Perseus isn't an isolated case and shows that considerable energy is propagating out from the central engine into the intracluster gas," said Dr. Andrew Fabian of Cambridge University, who led the team that worked on Perseus.

As a result, the birth of new stars in those clusters has virtually halted. Dr. Peter Edmonds, another Harvard-Smithsonian astronomer who was not a member of either team, said in an e-mail message, "Billions or trillions of stars might be prevented from forming in M87 because of this black hole activity."

Such feedback activity from black holes, said Dr. Fabian and other astronomers, may be responsible for limiting the growth of galaxies. As the galaxy grows, the central black hole feeds and feeds from the accretion of gas, dust and smaller galaxies until its outbursts are strong enough to keep more material from falling into either the hole or the galaxy.

That kind of self-regulation, Dr. Loeb said, may explain a puzzle noted a few years ago. In 2000, work by two groups of astronomers, one led by Dr. Karl Gebhardt of the University of Texas, and another by Dr. Laura Ferrarese of Rutgers, found a mysterious correlation between the masses of the black holes and the masses of the galaxies in which they lived.

Bigger galaxies have larger gravitational fields and thus attract more material into their centers where the black holes feed, Dr. Loeb explained, and therefore black holes have to grow larger before their outbursts have enough oomph to hold off the gas falling into them.

But that view may be too simplistic, according to Dr. Anton Koekemoer of the Space Telescope Science Institute in Baltimore, who notes that the jets and outbursts from black holes actually seem to touch off the formation of stars by compressing interstellar gas along their boundaries, and to keep other gas from falling and condensing. "Both effects are going on at the same time," he said.

Just where these black holes came from is another problem.

Using Hubble as well as other telescopes, astronomers have inferred the presence of black holes, weighing up to a billion times the mass of the Sun, at the centers of most galaxies, including ones that existed only a billion years after the Big Bang itself. Earlier this year Stanford astronomers announced that they had found one with a mass of 10 billion times the mass of the Sun.

One theory is that these black holes are the remains of an early generation of very massive stars that condensed out of the primordial soup of hydrogen, 100 million to 200 million years after the Big Bang. They would rapidly burn out and explode, leaving behind a generation of "baby black holes," in Dr. Koekemoer's words, 100 or 200 times as massive as the Sun. These then grow by swallowing more gas or even each other. Dr. Loeb outlined an alternative scheme. Under certain circumstances, he explained, supermassive stars could be formed at the beginning. When they burned out and exploded these stars would leave behind black holes as much as 1,000 times as massive as the Sun.

"This would give you a jump-start," Dr. Loeb said.

Dr. Fabian said that how massive black holes could grow to large sizes without stifling their own growth was still an unsolved problem. Most of the growth of these black holes happened in the first few billion years of time, astronomers say, when the universe was dense with gas and the baby fragments of galaxies were furiously merging. The heyday of the quasars was about 10 billion years ago, when the universe was only four billion years old.

Since then the black holes of the universe have been relatively quiescent, including the one in our own Milky Way galaxy, only occasionally kicking up their heels in outbursts like the ones in M87 that are nonetheless and perhaps fortunately only a shadow of the energies of the quasars.

"A big black hole is kind of like a spider," Dr. Koekemoer said. "Most of the time it sits at the center of the galaxy doing nothing. Then a bug comes by. When it eats a bug, there is a burst of activity."

In the case of black holes, the bugs could be little galaxies, like the Milky Way's satellite, the Large Magellanic Cloud. And the result perhaps could be a chirp from our own resident black hole.

"If the Milky Way galaxy swallows the Large Magellanic Cloud, the black hole will light up," Dr. Koekemoer explained, adding, "It's been hungry a long time."

Gravity is an attractive force. When objects fall into a gravitational field, they are pulled toward the source of that gravity. But scientists speculate that there may also be a repulsive force in the universe, pushing objects away. This theory was given credence when it was revealed that the universe, after slowing down under gravity like a ball rolling up a hill, began to speed up about 7 billion years ago. The only explanation for this speeding up is dark energy.

Unlike gravity, dark energy grows stronger the farther two objects are apart. This is because dark energy exists in the vacuum of space. So, the more space between objects means the more dark energy there is.

While physicists don't know exactly what dark energy is, they are certain that understanding it will provide crucial clues in the quest to determine if the universe will someday fly apart, expand forever, or implode if dark energy suddenly flips and becomes attractive.

In "Dark Energy Fills the Cosmos," Paul Preuss studies how the largest example of the conservation of energy and momentum we know of—the expansion or contraction of the universe—can be affected by an energy we can neither detect nor calculate. —RV

"Dark Energy Fills the Cosmos"
by Paul Preuss
Berkeley Lab Research Review, June 1, 1999

In an article titled "The Cosmic Triangle: Revealing the State of the Universe," which appears in the May 28, 1999 issue of the journal *Science*, a group of cosmologists and physicists from Princeton University and Lawrence Berkeley National Laboratory survey the wide range of evidence which, they write, "is forcing us to consider the possibility that some cosmic dark energy exists that opposes the self-attraction of matter and causes the expansion of the universe to accelerate."

Dark energy is hardly science fiction, although no less intriguing and full of mystery for being real science.

"The universe is made mostly of dark matter and dark energy," says Saul Perlmutter, leader of the Supernova Cosmology Project headquartered at Berkeley Lab, "and we don't know what either of them is." He credits University of Chicago cosmologist Michael Turner with coining the phrase "dark energy" in an article they wrote together with Martin White of the University of Illinois for *Physical Review Letters*.

In the May 28 *Science* article, Perlmutter and Neta Bahcall, Jeremiah Ostriker, and Paul Steinhardt of Princeton use the concept of dark energy in discussing their graphic approach to understanding the past, present, and future status of the universe. The Cosmic Triangle is the authors' way of presenting the major questions cosmology must answer: "How much matter is in the universe? Is the expansion rate slowing down or speeding up? And, is the universe flat?"

The possible answers are values for three terms in an equation that describes the evolution of the universe according to the general theory of relativity. By plotting the best experimental observations and estimates within the triangle, scientists can make preliminary choices among competing models.

The mass density of the universe is estimated by deriving the ratio of visible light to mass in large systems such as clusters of galaxies, and in several other ways. For several decades the evidence has been building that mass density is low and that most of the matter in the universe is dark.

Changes in expansion rate are estimated by comparing the redshifts of distant galaxies with the apparent brightness of Type 1a supernovae found in them. These measurements suggest that the expansion of the universe is accelerating.

Curvature is estimated from measurements of the anisotropy (temperature fluctuation) of the cosmic microwave background radiation (CMB), a remnant of the Big Bang. Although uncertainty is large, current results suggest a flat universe.

The Cosmic Triangle eliminates some popular models, such as a high-density universe that is slowing down and will eventually recollapse, as well as a nearly empty universe with no dark energy and low mass. While the evidence from galactic clusters shows that mass density is low, supernova evidence for acceleration shows that dark energy must be abundant.

"These two legs of the Cosmic Triangle agree with the evidence from the CMB that the universe is flat," Perlmutter says, adding that "this is a remarkable agreement for these early days of empirical cosmology."

Thus the Cosmic Triangle suggests that the standard inflationary scenario is on the right track: one of its key predictions is a flat universe.

Various types of dark energy have been proposed, including a cosmic field associated with inflation; a different, low-energy field dubbed "quintessence"; and the cosmological constant, or vacuum energy of empty space. Unlike Einstein's famous fudge factor, the cosmological constant in its present incarnation doesn't delicately (and artificially) balance gravity in order to maintain a static universe; instead, it has "negative pressure" that causes expansion to accelerate.

"The term Cosmic Triangle sounds kind of New Agey," says Perlmutter, "but it's a good way to portray the quantities in these comparisons, and it's fun for people who like to plot the possibilities"—an evolving task that, among other choices, will require finding an answer to "the most provocative and profound" issue of all, the nature of cosmic dark energy.

The Berkeley Lab is a U.S. Department of Energy national laboratory located in Berkeley, California. It conducts unclassified scientific research and is managed by the University of California.

Reprinted with permission from Paul Preuss.

Launched by NASA in 2004, after more than two decades of development, the Earth-orbiting satellite Gravity Probe B is built exclusively to test whether and how the spinning Earth twists space-time around itself.

Albert Einstein described space-time as being warped by the gravity of Earth, stars, and anything possessing mass in space. When rotating matter causes space-time to spin around it, the effect is called frame dragging. These measurements of how matter warps space-time to produce gravity may allow physicists to better understand black holes and perhaps find evidence of new forces in the universe.

If the angular momentum of Earth couples with the space around it, it would put a drag on Earth's rotation. This would affect Earth's position relative to the background stars. Frame-dragging is predicted to cause Earth's spin axis to wobble, or precess, by a very tiny amount. If Gravity Probe B discovers that

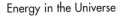

space-time is being dragged by the rotation of Earth, then any wobble of Earth's axis would be a natural result of the conservation of energy and momentum.

In "Gravity Probe to Give Einstein High-Precision Test," Charles Seife explores how a simple principle such as the conservation of energy and momentum can apply to a concept as advanced as space-time. —RV

"Gravity Probe to Give Einstein High-Precision Test"
by Charles Seife
Science, April 16, 2004

When ships, satellites, and spacecraft need a stationary point to steer by, they take aim at the stars. Gravity Probe B (GP-B) is no exception. In this case, though, it would be more appropriate for the satellite to guide the guide star.

The $700 million satellite is about to make a measurement so precise that the infinitesimal drift of its guide star—a binary in the constellation Pegasus—would ruin the experiment. To orient the craft, astronomers on the ground will have to measure the star's motion and take it into account. Only then can GP-B perform its mission: to measure an as-yet-unseen consequence of Einstein's theory of general relativity. The incredible precision needed has made the satellite expensive and controversial.

"This test of general relativity is very simple in concept, but when you get down to the technical details, excessive perseverance was needed, to say the least," says co-principal-investigator Brad Parkinson, an aerospace engineer at Stanford University in California.

GP-B is NASA's oldest experimental project; it was proposed in 1961 by Stanford scientists and received its first NASA funding 3 years later. Its roots go back to 1915, when Einstein combined space and time into a mathematical object that behaves like a rubber sheet. A massive object such as a star or a planet sitting on the sheet creates a dimple. A spacecraft floating near that object would tend to fall into the dimple—attraction that we perceive as gravity.

Two consequences of that theory, the warping of space and the warping of time, have been measured with great precision. In 1976, for example, GP-A tested how a 2-hour suborbital rocket flight altered a sensitive atomic clock. But a third, more subtle effect has eluded physicists. "The spinning of the Earth or the sun or other massive body drags spacetime along with it, something we have never seen in any definitive way," says Kip Thorne, a theorist at the California Institute of Technology in Pasadena. This so-called frame-dragging effect is the reason for GP-B.

GP-B is a very sensitive measurer of twist. Its heart is a concrete-mixer-sized Thermos bottle filled with liquid helium. Inside the Thermos are four incredibly smooth golf-ball-sized quartz spheres—the most nearly perfect spherical objects ever created by humans—each of which is set spinning around its axis 10,000 times a minute by carefully controlled squirts of helium. These spheres act as gyroscopes that, absent external influences, will always point in the same direction. "The gyros are 1 million times better than the best inertial navigation gyroscopes," says Stanford physicist Francis Everitt, co-PI of the GP-B mission.

As the spinning Earth drags spacetime along with it, the satellite's gyroscopes—themselves embedded in spacetime—will twist a bit as well. By keeping a careful watch on the gyroscopes' orientation with respect to the (corrected) guide star, scientists can deduce whether this frame-dragging effect changes the direction in which the gyroscopes point. (Scientists will also have to correct for skewing due to the warping of space-time by Earth. This "geodetic effect" is actually much greater than the twist due to frame dragging.) The expected change in angle is so tiny—41 thousandths of an arc second, roughly the breadth of a penny in Los Angeles as viewed by an observer in Washington, D.C.—that a small hiccup in the satellite or a flaw in the gyroscope would wipe out any hope of seeing the frame-dragging effect.

Such a finely tuned instrument is expensive, and GP-B's hefty price tag almost doomed it several times—especially because it is designed to verify a theory almost nobody doubts. Indeed, it had to fight for its survival up to the last minute; cost overruns and failed engineering tests made NASA officials consider scrapping the whole project. And if the satellite fails, there's no plan to replace it.

But if GP-B does fail, physicists might be able to spot frame dragging in other ways. In the late 1990s, x-ray astronomers thought that they saw hints of the effect in the swirling clouds of infalling gas around massive spinning neutron stars and black holes. Each disk-shaped cloud acts something like a gyroscope; the frame-dragging effect would cause the disk to wobble around the black hole, creating fluctuations in the x-rays that stream from those disks. Frame dragging could explain the observed fluctuations, says Wei Cui, an astronomer at Purdue University in West Lafayette, Indiana—but so could other models that don't invoke it, and it's unlikely that x-ray astronomers will get a definitive answer anytime soon. "This is the difference between this line of work and what Gravity Probe B will measure," he says. "That will be a direct measurement."

Another possibility would be to add a third space-craft to a pair of existing satellites known as LAGEOS. Scientists bounce lasers off these satellites to make precise measurements of the motion of tectonic plates. Frame dragging should shift the satellites' orbits, which themselves act like giant gyroscopes. So by measuring the orbits with great precision and accounting for variations in Earth's gravitational field, "you should see [frame dragging]—not at GP-B precision, but good enough," says Thorne.

LAGEOS could come in handy as a reality check if GP-B's results don't match Einstein's theory—an outcome few expect. "If it's not agreeing with general relativity, there will be extreme excitement in the community," says Thorne.

With luck, GP-B should yield a result in a little more than 18 months. Says Anne Kinney, director of NASA's astronomy and physics division, "My expectation is that it will be in all the textbooks."

Reprinted with permission from Seife, Charles, "Gravity Probe to Give Einstein High-Precision Test," *Science* 304:385 (2004). © 2004 AAAS.

A perplexing puzzle in science is that the universe is biased in favor of matter over so-called anti-matter. Antimatter is just like normal matter except that with antimatter, subatomic particles have the opposite electrical charges than those of normal matter. It's sort of like looking into a mirror and waving your left hand. The mirror image makes it look like you're waving your right hand.

When the universe was born in the big bang, it follows there should have been a perfectly equal mix of normal matter and antimatter. The big problem is that when matter and antimatter combine they cancel each other's electrical charge and the mass of each particle is converted to photons of energy. So the newborn universe should have converted all of its mass to energy through matter-antimatter annihilations.

The universe did convert a lot of its mass to energy. For every hydrogen atom in space there are 50 billion photons from the matter-antimatter annihilations after the big bang. But the fact that atoms exist at all means normal matter particles outnumbered antimatter particles by a razor-thin margin. To try and briefly replicate the conditions that existed shortly after the big bang, physicists smashed beams of particles together as described in the following article. They did this to discover the underlying cause for this asymmetry in nature. —RV

"Accelerator Gets Set to Explore Cosmic Bias"
by Andrew Watson
Science, August 7, 1998

An understanding of why the universe is biased in favor of matter may have come a step closer with a burst of collisions in a particle accelerator that has a bias of its own. Called the Asymmetric B Factory and based at the Stanford Linear Accelerator Center (SLAC), the machine collides a beam of electrons, accelerated in a ring 2200 meters around, with positrons, their anti-matter partners, accelerated to lower energies in a second ring of the same size. The collisions spawn B mesons, particles containing heavy bottom quarks, and the energy mismatch flings the B's off to one side for study. On 23 July, just days after the positron ring was completed, the two rings collided particles for the first time—a critical step in the long process of getting this novel facility up and running, which should be completed early next year.

"We're very excited about what we have managed to do," says project leader Jonathan Dorfan. "It's definitely a milestone," agrees George Brandenburg of a competing facility, CESR, the Cornell Electron-Positron Storage Ring. The B mesons made in the Stanford machine, CESR, and other colliders around the world should enable physicists to probe a phenomenon called CP violation, a subtle effect that distinguishes matter from antimatter and could explain why we live in a matter-dominated universe. The asymmetric Stanford machine could offer an especially sharp view of the phenomenon, because it boosts the short-lived B mesons to a large fraction of the speed of light, extending their lifetime through the time dilation predicted by Einstein's theory of relativity.

The new machine, built on time and on budget at a cost of $177 million, uses electron and positron beams from the existing SLAC linear accelerator. It stores the 9.0-billion-electron-volt (GeV) electrons in the old, rebuilt PEP ring, while a new ring stores the lower energy, 3.1 –GeY positron beam. The two superbright beams are brought into collision at a single crossing point, where the BaBar detector, now nearing completion, will watch for the creation and subsequent decay of about 100 million B mesons per year.

"The asymmetric energies make the design of the interaction region very complicated," says SLAC's John Seeman. The challenge, Dorfan explains, was designing a set of magnetic optics that can handle two beams of different energies simultaneously. The payoff, he believes, will be a better understanding of the symmetry between matter and antimatter, and why it breaks down.

In almost all particle interactions, matter and antimatter show a basic equivalence, CP symmetry. CP symmetry holds that the behavior of a set of particles and that of the matching antiparticles look identical—one system is a mirror-image of the other, with all the particle spins reversed. But, mysteriously, some exotic particle systems violate CP symmetry. "CP violation is one of the remaining enigmas of the standard model of particle physics," says Andreas Schwarz at the DESY accelerator center in Germany. It "can be linked to the very fact that matter dominates over antimatter in the universe."

B mesons, containing either a bottom quark or its antiparticle, are thought to show especially strong CP violation when they decay, making them ideal for probing this gray area in particle physics. That has spurred a worldwide surge of interest in accelerators that can mass-produce B mesons. Cornell, which lost out to SLAC 5 years ago in a competition for government funding for an asymmetric collider, will upgrade both the CESR accelerator and its CLEO detector in the middle of next year. DESY has a B meson project of its own, says Schwarz. And across the Pacific the sun is rising on the world's other asymmetric B factory, under construction at KEK, the Japanese high-energy physics lab near Tokyo, which is likely to produce its first collisions by the end of the year.

For now, Dorfan and his team are still coaxing their new machine to its full brightness and learning how to operate it efficiently. "We're not about to start physics next week," says Dorfan. At about the end of the year, the 1,000-ton BaBar detector will be slotted into place, and by next spring the machine will begin exploring the universe's fundamental bias.

Reprinted with permission from Watson, Andrew, "Accelerator Gets Set to Explore Cosmic Bias," *Science* 281:764–765 (1998). © 1998 AAAS.

Einstein described the universe essentially as a sheet of space and time called spacetime. Einstein's theory of general relativity predicts that cataclysmic events release energy that ripples across this boundless sheet. These ripples are called gravity waves.

Scientists believe gravity waves are common throughout the universe and are now developing the technology to detect them. The Laser Interferometer Gravitational-Wave Observatory (LIGO) in Louisiana and its recently completed twin in Washington State may be able to detect and measure these faint signals and, at the same time, test fundamental predictions of physics.

A lot of the problem in detecting gravity waves, though, is conservation of momentum. Conservation of momentum means that gravity waves basically cancel each other out. However, dense compact objects, like black holes or neutron stars, radiate gravitationally because they spiral in on each other. The kinetic energy generated by this motion of two massive bodies has to go somewhere. This is a special situation in which the motions of two bodies cause energy to be lost from the system in the form of gravitational waves.

In this article, Marcia Bartusiak studies how gravity waves are a unique example of the conservation of energy and momentum. —RV

"Catch a Gravity Wave"
by Marcia Bartusiak
Astronomy, October 2000

Two sprawling observatories in Washington and Louisiana will test one of Einstein's great theoretical predictions.

The Hanford Nuclear Reservation, currently the nation's prime repository for nuclear waste, sprawls over hundreds of square miles of scrub desert in south-central Washington state. The nearest town, Richland, is 10 miles away. At a key intersection, the road signs direct travelers to either continue west or turn south. There is no sign at all to explain the highway going north, the entrance to the reservation. It is a leftover habit from Hanford's many years as a national secret during World War II.

Five miles down that desolate road resides the Laser Interferometer Gravitational-Wave Observatory operated by the California Institute of Technology and the Massachusetts Institute of Technology. Those in the know simply call it LIGO (pronounced LIE-go). It is a rent-free guest on the Hanford site. Standing alone on the vast plain, a landscape long ago carved flat by the immense outflow of an ancient glacial lake, the complex resembles either a tasteful warehouse or a modern art museum inexplicably placed in the middle of nowhere. An exact duplicate, painted in the same hues of cream, blue, and silver gray, can be found in the pine forests of Livingston Parish in Louisiana, outside Baton Rouge. Together, they form an astronomical tool of the 21st century, a detector like no other before it.

The signals these two observatories seek are waves of gravitational radiation, or more simply gravity waves, as they are better known in the popular media. Electromagnetic waves, be they visible light, infrared light, or radio waves, are produced by molecules, atoms, or electrons and generally reveal a celestial object's physical condition—how hot it is, how old it is, or what it is made of. Gravity waves will not convey such information. Instead, they will tell us about the motions of massive celestial objects. "It's both an exciting and overpowering change," says Gary Sanders, LIGO's deputy director. "There's almost a romantic attraction, this chance to look at a whole new window of the universe."

Spacequakes

Gravity waves are literally quakes in spacetime that emanate from the most violent events the universe has to offer—a once blazing star burning out and going supernova, the dizzying spin of neutron stars, or the cagey dance of two black holes whirling around each other, approaching closer and closer until they merge. Gravity waves will tell scientists how large amounts of matter move, twirl, and collide throughout the universe. Eventually, this new method of examining the cosmos may even record the remnant rumble of the first nanosecond of creation, the remains of the ultimate spacetime jolt of the Big Bang itself.

Inside LIGO's main halls, at both Hanford and Livingston, the ambiance is almost reverential, akin to the response one might feel inside a darkened telescope dome. But this astronomical venture is vastly different. There are no windows to spy on the universe. Instead, two 4-foot-wide tubes at right angles to each other extend out into the countryside for 2.5 miles (4 kilometers). Together, these arms form a giant L in the landscape. The tubes resemble oil pipelines, although they can't be seen directly. Six-inch-thick concrete covers protect them from the wind and rain. In Louisiana, the concrete has also stopped occasional stray bullets during hunting season. A hit could be devastating because the pipes are as empty of air as the vacuum of space. Indeed, they surround the largest artificial vacuum in the world.

These gravity-wave observatories are firmly planted on cosmos firma, awaiting their first rumbles, vibrations predicted by Albert Einstein 84 years ago. "The worship of Einstein is the only reason we're here," says Rainer Weiss of MIT, one of LIGO's founding fathers. "If you go to Congress and tell them you're going to try to show that Heisenberg's uncertainty principle is not quite right, you run into blank stares. But if you say you're measuring something that's proving or disproving Einstein's theory, then all sorts of doors open. There's a mystique."

Einstein unleashed a revolution that altered the commonplace notions of space and time. His general theory of relativity showed that matter, space, and time are linked, producing the force known as gravity. Space and time are joined together into an entity known as spacetime, whose geometry is determined by the matter around it. According to general relativity, stars and other massive bodies dimple the spacetime around them, much the way a bowling ball creates a depression in an elastic mat. Planets and comets are attracted to the star because they follow the curved spacetime highway carved out by the stellar orb.

When it was first introduced in 1915, general relativity was hailed as a momentous conceptual achievement but thought to have little practical importance. How times have changed. Global Positioning Satellites, used regularly by hikers, sailors, pilots, and soldiers to keep track of their locations, continually require general relativistic corrections to keep in sync. Moreover, astronomers discovered intriguing celestial objects such as pulsars, quasars, and black holes that they could be understood only through the physics of general relativity. And yet the story of general relativity remains incomplete.

A major prediction of general relativity still awaits direct observational confirmation: gravitational waves. Einstein first mentioned them in 1916. He recognized that just as radio waves are generated when electrons travel up and down an antenna, gravity waves should be produced when masses move about. To understand this phenomenon, imagine one of the most violent events the universe has to offer—two supermassive black holes crashing into each other in the center of our galaxy. When this happens, space is shaken—and shaken hard. Such a colossal collision would send out a spacequake that surges through the cosmos at the speed of light. Its waves would not travel through space in the manner a light wave propagates. Rather, they would be an agitation of space itself. The waves would alternately compress and extend the fabric of spacetime.

Such waves would be deadly near the crash site. They would stretch a 6-foot man to 12 feet and within a millisecond squeeze him to three, before stretching him out once again. Any planets in the vicinity would be torn asunder. Fortunately, by the time such waves reached Earth, this cosmic tsunami would be reduced to a subatomic flutter. Were such gravity waves to hit this page, they would be so weak that they would squeeze and stretch the sheet's dimensions by a distance thousands of times smaller than the size of a proton.

Almost no one doubts that gravitational waves exist, for there is already powerful evidence they are real. Two neutron stars in our galaxy are rapidly orbiting each other, drawing closer and closer together. The rate of their orbital decay—about three feet per year—is just the change physicists expect if this binary pair is losing orbital energy in the form of gravitational waves. Joseph Taylor and Russell Hulse won the Nobel Prize in 1993 for this discovery. Direct reception of a wave, though, would offer the ultimate proof and provide astronomers with one of the most radical new tools to explore the heavens in four centuries. This explains the motivation to construct LIGO, as well as similar instruments of varying sizes in Italy, Germany, and Japan.

The Gong Show

This entire endeavor began modestly in the 1960s as one man's quixotic quest. University of Maryland physicist Joseph Weber cleverly surmised that a burst of gravitational energy should set a large cylindrical bar of aluminum vibrating, much like a gong continuing to ring after being struck, though far more weakly. When he reported a detection in 1969, others around the world quickly constructed bar antennae. While most physicists remained highly skeptical of Weber's detections, he initiated a new branch of physics that has never diminished.

The seeds of LIGO, a scheme different from Weber's, can be traced to a classroom exercise three decades ago. To teach the concept of gravity waves during a general relativity course at MIT, Weiss asked his students to envision three mirrors suspended above the ground, their orientation forming the shape of an L. One mirror would be in the corner, the others at each end. Weiss understood that as a gravity wave travels it does two things: The wave compresses space in one direction—say, north/south—while simultaneously expanding it in the perpendicular direction—east/west. A gravity wave coming straight down on this L-shaped set-up would squeeze one of the arms so the mirrors would be closer together, while spreading the mirrors in the other arm farther apart. A millisecond later, as the gravity wave continues onward, this effect would reverse, with the compressed arm expanding and the expanding arm contracting. Weiss was rediscovering an idea that Weber and others had thought of earlier, but Weiss carried out a detailed study that envisioned nearly all the crucial pieces of the observatories now coming on line.

Weiss figured that a laser beam, bouncing back and forth between the mirrors at each end of the L, could track a gravity wave's expand/contract flutters. The light would enter the corner of the L. A beam splitter would split the light into two beams, each directed down an arm. After multiple reflections off the mirrors, the beams could be recombined, at which time they interfere with each other (hence the term "interferometry"). The beams could be initially set so that their waves arrive out of phase. In other words, when added together, the waves from both arms would cancel each other out. When the crest of the light wave in one beam is added to the trough of the light wave in the other beam, the result is darkness, like adding 1 and –1 to get zero. But if a gravity wave causes the arms to expand or contract, the two laser beams would travel slightly different distances. In that case, the recombined beams will be more in phase and would thus produce some light. The gravity wave would be spotted in those light changes.

Weiss's concept caught on because it had a distinct advantage. A bar antenna can be tuned to only one gravity-wave frequency (as if it were a radio that could pick up only one station). A laser interferometer, on the other hand, is like a broad-band radio. It can detect a wide range of frequencies, making it more versatile for astronomy. Weber's protegé Robert Forward operated the first prototype, a small tabletop instrument, in 1972 at the Hughes Research Laboratories in California. Pioneering groups in Scotland and Germany went on to build interferometers with longer arms, making technological breakthroughs that at last allowed laser interferometry to surpass the bars in sensitivity. A turning point came in 1979 when Caltech lured the Scottish interferometry wizard Ronald Drever to its campus to build an instrument with 40-meter arms, the longest in its day.

From Test Beds to Telescopes

But these were all test beds, not true gravity-wave telescopes. Detecting spacetime tremors requires interferometers with arms miles in length. The subatomic expansions and contractions are easier to measure over long distances. The longer the armspan, the greater the effect. When MIT joined forces with Caltech in 1983, they planned to build two large observatories.

But their funding did not arrive for nearly a decade. With no guarantee that a gravity wave would be detected, many astronomers and physicists waged a long, hard campaign against LIGO, declaring that the money would be better spent on surer scientific quests. But the potential of the science—not to mention strong politicking—eventually overrode those concerns.

With a final construction cost of $292 million (making LIGO the most expensive project ever funded by the National Science Foundation), the Hanford and Livingston, observatories are separated by nearly 1,900 miles (3,000 km). The two are more like fraternal than identical twins. The Hanford facility actually houses two interferometers, which operate side by side through the arms. There is a full-length detector of 2.5 miles, as well as one half as long. The Livingston observatory has only the full-length interferometer. Each observatory, though, follows the same principles first established by Weiss, Drever, and others some three decades ago.

The mirrors, now two in each arm, are made of fused silica. Ten inches wide and four inches thick, each 22-pound (10-kg) cylindrical disk is polished to a smoothness that does not vary by more than 30-billionths of an inch. "If Earth were that smooth," notes LIGO's Gari Lynn Billingsley, who monitored the mirrors' production, "then the average mountain would not rise more than an inch." Such smoothness is a must for the light to be reflected over and over again to extreme accuracy. Each mirror is balanced on a single steel wire that is attached to a gallows-like frame. This support, in turn, rests on an isolation platform, not unlike a car's suspension system, to reduce seismic jitters by a millionfold.

Two observatories are needed to rule out local disturbances that might mimic a gravity wave at any one site, such as a passing garbage truck or seismic tremors. A gravity wave will pass through both observatories within 10 milliseconds of each other. In addition, the shape and size of the wave should be identical in both places.

LIGO will be most receptive to frequencies from 100 to 3,000 hertz, which is coincidentally the same frequencies our ears pick up as sound. You could actually listen to the signal, once it is electronically recorded. "It sounds like a hiss," notes LIGO's Albert Lazzarini. "Actually, it's a hiss with warbles in it due to the suspension. It's eerie, in some ways like whale songs." Gravity waves will at last be adding sound to our cosmic senses.

Computers, not ears, though, will be sifting through LIGO's data. The technique will be similar to the way in which military sonar experts search for the distinctive sound of a submarine amid the many noises of the sea. Essentially, as the data stream comes in, it will be compared to a "template," a theoretical prediction of what a gravity-wave signal might look like. Take, for example, the case of two neutron stars spiraling into each other. According to computer simulations, this system can produce many possible wave patterns because the signal depends on both the masses of the neutron stars and their orientation as viewed from Earth. To do a proper search, LIGO will have to continually compare its stream of data against some 20,000 to 30,000 possible signal patterns worked out by theorists.

Neutron star collisions may be the bread and butter of LIGO's trade. Once the detectors are sensitive enough to see hundreds of millions of light-years beyond Earth, they may detect a few mergers per year. LIGO will register the binary's final minutes, a sort of whine that rapidly rises in pitch, like the sound of a swiftly approaching ambulance siren, as the two city-sized balls of dense matter spiral into each other.

The biggest prize of all will be two black holes colliding. As the twirling holes are about to meet, spiraling inward faster and faster at speeds close to that of light, computer models predict that the whine will turn into a chirp, a birdlike trill that races up the scales in a matter of seconds. A cymbal-like crash, a mere millisecond in length, heralds the final collision and merger. The two black holes become one. A ring down, akin to the diminishing tone of a struck gong, follows as the new black hole swirls around like the fearsome tornado in *The Wizard of Oz*, wobbles a bit, and then settles down. Such a sighting would be the first direct evidence that black holes truly exist.

Other potential signals include the explosive burst of an asymmetric supernova, a murmur from the Big Bang itself, and the steady beat from a rotating neutron star. "But what if the strongest gravitational-wave signal," asks Lazzarini, "is a belch or burp that arrives sporadically? Then what? You have to assure yourself it wasn't just an amplifier problem or a bad wire." Those sorts of signals, the unexpected or irregular, will be the most difficult of all, "but they're also where the biggest surprises and most profound discoveries may lie," adds Lazzarini.

First Light

When new optical telescopes come on line, there is usually a celebratory "first light event, the moment when the Instrumentation is turned on and the first picture taken. LIGO's construction was completed last November, but its initiation was not so dramatic. Because its engineering and optics are so complex, LIGO will require a few years for its initial shakedown and calibration before all three interferometers—the two at Hanford, the other in Louisiana—can work in concert with one another. Then and only then can the search for gravity waves really begin, perhaps by late 2002.

LIGO researchers concede that their first detectors may not register a thing. For its critics, that made LIGO technologically unjustifiable and premature. LIGO, however, was built on the belief that scientists and engineers couldn't have found solutions without first building a full-sized facility to carry out the needed tests. At first, the two interferometers will be able to detect a change in spacetime as small as a millionth trillionth of a meter. Even then, the observatories will have only a small chance at observing an event. Over the years, upgrades will increase sensitivities more than tenfold, enabling LIGO to "feel" spacetime rumbles emanating from a variety of sources hundreds of millions or even billions of light-years distant. An advanced LIGO might register an event a day.

But what keeps LIGO researchers at work when no signal is guaranteed? "People take pleasure in solving the technical challenges," answers physicist Peter Saulson of Syracuse University, "much the way medieval cathedral builders continued working knowing they might not see the finished church. But if there wasn't a fighting chance to see a gravity wave during my career, I wouldn't be in this field. If you do this, you have the right stuff."

5

Black Holes and Neutron Stars

Gamma-ray bursts are spectacular releases of energy that can outshine everything else in their vicinity. A burst is recorded by astronomers from a random part of the sky at least once a day. The popular thinking now is that these bursts come from so-called hypernovas. Hypernovas are stars at least ten times our Sun's mass that undergo titanic explosions at the end of their lives. However, another source of gamma-ray bursts may be from small black holes that detonate like time bombs in our stellar neighborhood.

These short bursts come from a specific direction in our galaxy, suggesting they are local phenomena. One theory is that they are the detonation of black holes formed during the big bang. It's predicted that black holes eventually "evaporate" by "leaking" mass back into space. This means that black holes abruptly end their lives in a violent burst of energy, releasing this energy back into the universe and, thus, conserving the amount of energy in the universe.

Here, Marcus Chown explores this new theory relating to the principle of the conservation of energy in our universe. —RV

"Black Holes 'Detonating All Over Our Galaxy'"
by Marcus Chown
New Scientist, **November 28, 2001**

Tiny black holes may be detonating like time bombs all over our cosmic backyard. The explosions could explain a class of unusual energy bursts that have been picked up here on Earth, say physicists in the US.

Gamma-ray bursts are spectacular releases of energy that for a few seconds can outshine everything else in the Universe. They can come from any part of the sky, and from this astronomers have concluded that they are produced at the very edge of the Universe, most likely in the super-bright fireballs created by the birth or merger of star-sized black holes.

But David Cline, Christina Matthey and Stanislaw Otwinowski of the University of California in Los Angeles say this is not true of bursts that last for less than 100 milliseconds, which make up 42 of the 3,000 bursts observed so far.

These short gamma-ray bursts don't come from all directions. Nor are they concentrated in the disc of our Galaxy or at its centre, as would be expected if they were associated with stars. But there is a hint of a concentration towards the Orion spiral arm of our Galaxy, the next spiral arm out from the Sun, and this, says Cline, "suggests they are local".

Hawking Radiation

Most gamma-ray bursts are quite varied. But the short bursts identified by Cline share the same characteristics, suggesting they are all caused by similar events. Cline suggests that we are seeing the detonation of microscopic black holes formed in the big bang.

Black holes are thought to end their lives in a violent burst of energy called Hawking radiation. The bigger their mass, the longer they survive before this happens. For black holes to be dying today, about 14 billion years after the big bang, they would have to have a mass of 100 million tones—about that of a small mountain— and have been created when the Universe was less than a billion-billion-billionth of a second old.

The researchers are preparing a paper on their work for the journal *Astroparticle Physics*. If they are right, every cube of space a few light years across in our cosmic neighbourhood could contain some 10 billion primordial black holes waiting to go off. This puts the closest hardly further away than Pluto.

Every year, in the same volume, a few will detonate, each with the energy of 100 billion one-megaton H-bombs. Dramatic as that sounds, we are quite safe, says Cline: "One would have to go off closer than the Sun to affect the Earth."

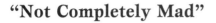

"Not Completely Mad"

Other astronomers are cautious about the theory. "The idea isn't completely mad," says Martin Rees of the University of Cambridge.

Roger Blandford of the California Institute of Technology in Pasadena says he has yet to be convinced that the short bursts are in a class of their own. "But Cline's proposal has the merit of being testable in the near future."

To gain more evidence, Cline and his team suggest looking more closely at the way the brightness changes during the bursts. Fluctuations that lasted a matter of nanoseconds would support the idea that the source is a very small object such as a primordial black hole.

Reprinted with permission from *New Scientist*.

Neutron stars are rapidly spinning crushed cores of exploded stars. Even though they are as big in diameter as a major city, neutron stars can spin thousands of times per second.

How do they spin so fast? When a star collapses, it must conserve angular momentum. This means that if the radius of the star shrinks, it must correspondingly increase its rate of rotation. This is analogous to an ice skater pulling his arms close to his body to spin faster.

But the rotational energy of a neutron star does not stay constant. Neutron stars slow down over time. What saps the angular momentum from a neutron star? The best explanation is a magnetic field. A magnetic field puts drag on a spinning neutron star, like a blender trying to mix a milk shake. The milk shake robs some of the blender's energy through drag and converts it to heat. Likewise, a neutron star's powerful magnetic field acts like the milk shake.

The magnetic field of a neutron star must be as strong as 100 trillion times the intensity of Earth's magnetic field in order to slow it down in a few thousand years. The magnetic drag is converted to heat energy, which raises the temperature of the neutron star's surface.

In this article, Robert Irion examines how the magnetic field of neutron stars illustrates the conservation of energy and momentum in an unprecedented way. —RV

"Crushed by Magnetism"
by Robert Irion
Science, April 23, 2004

Mutations are the spice of life, but the most freakish mutants usually die at a tender age. This biological rule holds true in astrophysics: Some of the strangest

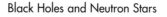

mutations in space create superenergetic but short-lived cousins of pulsars, called magnetars.

Like a pulsar, a magnetar is a neutron star forged at the center of a supernova when a massive star explodes. But something odd happens during a magnetar's birth. An unknown process—perhaps ultrafast rotation within the dying star's collapsing core—endows each magnetar with a crushing magnetic field. This magnetism, up to 1,000 times more intense than that of a typical pulsar, is the strongest known in space.

As the magnetic forces subside, they rupture the brittle crust of the neutron star and drive fierce bursts of gamma rays and x-rays. But the pyrotechnics takes a toll. The magnetism acts as a brake, grinding each magnetar to a near-halt within thousands of years and short-circuiting its spin power. In contrast, an ordinary pulsar can sweep the galaxy with rotation-powered beams of radio waves for millions of years.

Astrophysicists have found just 11 magnetars, but their brief lives and sporadic tantrums point to a far larger population that we can't see. "There probably are hundreds of thousands of these dead relics, undetected and undetectable, now spinning in our galaxy," says x-ray astronomer Chryssa Kouveliotou of NASA's Marshall Space Flight Center (MSFC) in Huntsville, Alabama. Indeed, some proponents think the objects might not be mutants at all but common offspring of supernovas. "It's quite possible that a majority of neutron stars are magnetars rather than radio pulsars," says astrophysicist Robert Duncan of the University of Texas, Austin.

A Hundred Billion MRI Scans

That's a grand claim, but Duncan and fellow theorist Christopher Thompson of the Canadian Institute for Theoretical Astrophysics in Toronto, Ontario, have swayed skeptics before. They first calculated that powerful magnetic fields could lace through newborn neutron stars in 1987, when Duncan was a postdoctoral researcher at Princeton University and Thompson was a graduate student. But their solution for the strengths of such fields—10^{15} gauss—was so startling that they weren't sure what to make of it for several years.

For perspective, Earth's global magnetic field is about 0.6 gauss. Magnetic resonance imagers for medical scans attain 10,000 gauss. Radio pulsars cluster around 10^{12} gauss, a deduction based on magnetism's gradual braking effect on their spins. Such fields are impressive, but a radio pulsar's main power comes from its rotation, not its magnetism. The magnetic fields act as conveyor belts to carry radiation spawned as the neutron star slows down and sheds rotational energy. No one expected the fields to soar much higher.

But Thompson and Duncan realized that ultra-strong fields could explain some mysteries. Notably, astrophysicists were puzzled by soft gamma repeaters (SGRs). These unidentified objects emitted erratic flares of soft gamma rays—a notch above the most piercing x-rays—then fell quiet. In 1979, an SGR in a neighboring galaxy unleashed a giant flare that packed as much energy into its first 0.2 seconds as the sun produces in 10,000 years. The source was close to the remains of a recent supernova. However, the flare ebbed and flowed just once every 8 seconds as it gradually subsided, seemingly far too slow to come from a pulsar.

The theorists postulated that the bursts arose from a slow-spinning neutron star that had spun breathtakingly fast at birth. Astrophysicists Adam Burrows of the University of Arizona in Tucson and James Lattimer of the State University of New York, Stony Brook, had shown that during a neutron star's first 10 seconds of existence, its hot nuclear fluid would convect about 100 times every second. If the neutron star whirled between 100 and 1000 times each second during those birth pangs, Thompson and Duncan calculated, it would spark a furious dynamo—a self-sustaining generator of an intense magnetic field, 10^{15} gauss and beyond.

Once magnetism suffuses the dense superfluid of a neutron star, it's tough to disperse. Still, the magnetic fields and the electric currents that support them try to shift into patterns that are less taut with pent-up energy. "The magnetic field is strongly wound up in a tight spiral inside the star," Thompson explains. "It is the progressive unwinding of the field that drives the [SGR] flares." Each shift strains the solid crust of the neutron star. At a critical point the crust snaps, creating faults that may span a kilometer. Once the surface cracks, the magnetic fields above it whip into new positions as well. The violent motions blast particles along the magnetic fields, triggering gamma rays and x-rays.

Duncan and Thompson published this scenario in 1992, discarding their initial "burstar" term for the more descriptive "magnetar." Three years later, they noted that the magnetic fields should confine a burst's energy in a fireball lasting a few minutes, exactly the pattern observed.

Still, their notions were too fantastic for most colleagues. As recently as January 1998, Duncan was relegated to the last talk of the last session at a meeting of the American Astronomical Society (AAS)—just after a speaker who explored alternatives to Einstein's general theory of relativity.

But later that year, observations won the day. First, a team led by Kouveliotou used NASA's Rossi X-ray Timing Explorer (RXTE) satellite to measure pulsations once every 7.47 seconds in an SGR with frequent outbursts. The periodic fluctuations were visible only during bright bursts; at other times the SGR did not emit ordinary pulsar-like beams. The object's rotational "clock" was slowing down by an astonishing 0.26 seconds per century—an effect that could result only from the strong drag of a magnetic field around 10^{15} gauss.

Then on 27 August 1998, a wave of gamma rays and x-rays more intense than the 1979 flare swept through the solar system. The source was an SGR across the Milky Way. Despite the distance, the radiation was powerful enough to affect radio transmissions on Earth by strongly ionizing the upper atmosphere. Slow, 5.16-second pulsations modulated the flare. Kouveliotou's team also studied it with RXTE to show that the SGR's spin decelerated at a magnetar-like clip.

With those findings, magnetars passed into mainstream science. Peers honored the work last year when Duncan, Thompson, and Kouveliotou jointly received the 2003 Bruno Rossi Prize, the top research award from the AAS High-Energy Astrophysics Division. It was a stark contrast to the theory's early years, Duncan recalls: "There was resistance, and a whole bunch of people thought it was crazy. But I view it all as a normal part of the scientific process."

Transients and Nuclear Bombs

In recent years, astronomers have broadened the magnetar family. Most now agree that objects called anomalous x-ray pulsars (AXPs), which pulsate slowly in x-rays but not in radio waves, are another flavor of magnetar. Astronomer Victoria Kaspi of McGill University in Montreal, Canada, and her colleagues have shown that AXPs can spew impulsive bursts, although not quite as vehemently as SGRs.

Curiously, the 11 known SGRs and AXPs all spin at nearly the same rate: between 5 and 12 seconds for each rotation. Magnetic fields stifle a young magnetar's spin so severely that its rotation stutters from a few milliseconds down to a few seconds within centuries—such a brief interval that astronomers would have to get lucky to see a furiously spinning magnetar. "And if they were active for more than a few thousand years, we'd expect to see some with periods of tens of seconds, but we don't," says astronomer Peter Woods of MSFC. "So it appears to be a very short life cycle when they are x-ray bright."

Two new studies to appear in the *Astrophysical Journal* suggest that magnetars are more common than their measly statistics indicate. In one report, astronomers led by Woods describe an AXP that flickered intensely for 4 hours in June 2002, then just as quickly faded. Similar outbursts elsewhere in the galaxy might go undetected by current instruments, says Woods, because telescopes that monitor the whole sky aren't yet sensitive enough. In another study, astronomers led by Alaa Ibrahim of NASA's Goddard Space Flight Center in Greenbelt, Maryland, exposed a "transient" magnetar. The object was too faint to attract attention throughout the 1990s, but it suddenly grew 100 times brighter in early 2003.

In their quiet states, these misbehaving magnetars bear some resemblance to faint sources of x-rays in supernova remnants, called central compact objects. They also look similar to another mysterious class of bodies called dim isolated neutron stars. Kaspi, a collaborator on both studies, agrees that the magnetar family tree may include some of these branches. "Dim isolated neutron stars could be dead magnetars with some residual heat," she says. "I think the numbers are consistent with half the neutron star population being born as magnetars." But better counts—and a firmer handle on the strengths of magnetic fields—are needed before anyone accepts that logic.

On the theoretical side, several groups are probing possible links between magnetars and gamma ray bursts (GRBs), the most energetic explosions in the cosmos. Many astrophysicists now think the most viable triggers of long-duration GRBs, lasting seconds to minutes, are powerful supernovas that create newborn black holes. However, a magnetically dominated wind from a new magnetar makes more sense as a coherent driving force, says astrophysicist Maxim Lyutikov of McGill University. "The dissipation of magnetic energy can be very efficient," he notes. In contrast, blasts of matter from close to a black hole might lose too much energy within violent shocks.

In related work, modeling by Hubble postdoctoral fellow Todd Thompson of the University of California, Berkeley, shows that a brand-new magnetar will sling matter into space along stiff magnetic "spokes" at nearly the speed of light. This outpouring of mass expels so much momentum that if the magnetar spins 1000 times per second at birth, it takes merely 10 seconds to slam the brakes down to about 300 spins per second. That deceleration releases a whopping 90% of the object's energy. Thompson thinks all that energy can propel a hyperenergetic supernova or, under the right conditions, a GRB. The heaviest elements in nature could arise in this turbulent setting as well, Thompson adds. Astrophysicists haven't yet identified a convincing site for the "r-process," the creation of heavy atomic nuclei by rapid bombardment with a fierce wind of neutrons. Ultrastrong magnetic fields might keep a hot bath of neutrons and protons close enough to a new magnetar to push element synthesis up the periodic table to uranium and beyond.

Duncan, advocate of all things magnetar, loves the idea. "It's possible that all elements heavier than bismuth are synthesized in magnetar winds," he says. "If that's true, nuclear bombs and reactors are running on magnetar energy." Since supernovas supply the iron in our blood, it's only fair that magnetars get in on the action as well.

In the mid-1990s, astronomers confirmed the existence of supermassive holes at the centers of various galaxies. These supermassive black holes can be millions and billions of times the mass of our Sun and serve as the anchors for these massive galaxies.

Recently discovered intermediate-mass black holes are the missing link in understanding how small black holes may come together and combine their energy to build the supermassive black holes that exist in the centers of galaxies. Intermediate-mass black holes are thousands of times our Sun's mass. They are found in globular star clusters, which are giant swarms of hundreds of thousands of stars.

In "The Missing Black Hole Link," Nate McCrady explains how scientists believe these intermediate-mass black holes may be the building blocks that form supermassive black holes. According to this theory, intermediate-mass black holes collide in a process called mass segregation. In this process, intermediate-mass black holes exchange momentum with small stars. The smaller stars pick up speed as they orbit inside a galaxy, and the black hole loses momentum to fall ever deeper toward the center of a galaxy. —RV

From "The Missing Black Hole Link"
by Nate McCrady
Nature, April 15, 2004

A class of black holes of intermediate mass is expected but has never been detected. The suggestion that these beasts might lurk behind powerful X-ray sources in nearby galaxies is now strengthened.

Black holes are known to exist in two mass regimes: those between two and ten times the mass of the Sun, known as stellar-mass black holes and formed from the collapse of the most massive stars; and those between a million and a billion times the mass of the Sun, the "supermassive" black holes. Such behemoths, including the one at the centre of the Milky Way,[1] are the engines powering quasars and active galactic nuclei. Between the two extremes are intermediate-mass black holes, although these have never been detected unambiguously. Observations from NASA's Chandra space observatory have stoked the debate over their existence. The images show extremely luminous, compact X-ray sources lurking in and around star clusters in nearby galaxies—sources that might be associated with intermediate-mass black holes.

Central to the discussion is the lack of a credible mechanism by which these objects could have formed. But dynamical simulations . . . show that stellar collisions in dense star clusters could run away and lead to the formation of an intermediate-mass black hole at the cluster core. This process is particularly intriguing because the accretion of such black holes early in the galaxy-formation process is a crucial step in the formation of supermassive black holes at galaxy centres.

The nature of "ultraluminous X-ray sources" (ULXs), identified in high-resolution Chandra images, is a key question in the black-hole debate. Bright X-ray point sources in galaxies are generally either young remnants of supernovae, which fade over time, or the compact remnant of a massive star (a neutron star or a stellar-mass black hole). The latter shine as they accrete matter, typically from a companion star. The brightness of such an object generally cannot exceed the Eddington limit, which is the luminosity at which radiation pressure from escaping photons overcomes gravity and disperses the accreting material. ULXs are deemed "ultraluminous" because the isotropic luminosities implied by their measured fluxes exceed the Eddington limit for the largest black holes formed from single massive stars. If ULXs are actually black holes accreting matter, then their masses must fall in the 100 to 1,000 solar-mass range the missing intermediate-mass black holes.

Observations[3,4] indicate that ULXs tend to be located in or near star clusters in starburst galaxies, sites of very active star formation. This connection prompted the suggestion[5,6] that intermediate-mass black holes are formed in "super star clusters"—young, dense clusters 10 to 100 times more massive than the ancient globular clusters they closely resemble. The largest stars formed

in such clusters have masses 100 to 150 times that of the Sun, but they leave behind black holes of only 15 to 20 solar masses.

To form an intermediate-mass black hole, a mechanism other than star formation is required: Portegies Zwart *et al.*[2] propose runaway growth prompted by the collision of stars. In the field of a disk galaxy, outside clusters, collisions between stars are very unlikely, because their cross-sectional area is so small compared with the vast distances between them (galaxies are, in fact, far more common collision partners). Dense star clusters, however, are a different matter.[7] The most massive stars in a cluster tend to sink in towards the core, by transferring energy to lower-mass stars in a process known as mass segregation. Once the central density becomes high enough, collisions between high-mass stars can occur. But can these collisions create a "runaway star" that builds sufficient mass to beget a 100–1,000-solar-mass black hole, before the high-mass stars explode as supernovae?

Portegies Zwart *et al.* have used many-body simulations to examine the behaviour of a pair of young super star clusters[8] in the nearby starburst galaxy M82. One cluster, MGG 11, coincides spatially with the brightest ULX discovered so far, the luminosity of which corresponds to an intermediate-mass black hole of 300–900 solar masses.[9]

The authors' simulations indicate that, in this cluster, a runaway star could form on the necessary timescale. The result is tantalizing—this could well be how the building blocks of supermassive black holes formed.

Deep-space images from the Hubble Space Telescope indicate that galaxy mergers were common at early times in the history of the Universe, and the conditions in the centres of those merging galaxies might have resembled those seen in nearby starburst galaxies today. The link between ULXs and intermediate-mass black holes is, however, not conclusive. There are plausible alternative explanations for the high X-ray luminosities of ULXs, such as beaming[10] (the observed X-ray flux is emitted through a narrow opening angle rather than iso-tropically) and super-Eddington emission (attributed to "clumpy" accretion disks[11]). More high-resolution observations of super star clusters and ULXs, coupled with simulations of star-cluster dynamics, will ensure that the debate over intermediate-mass black holes continues.

Source Notes

1. Ghez. A. M., Morris, M., Becklin, E. E., Tanner, A. & Kremenek, T. *Nature* **407**, 349–351 (2000).
2. Portegies Zwart, S. F., Baumgardt, H., Hut, P., Makino, J. & McMillan, S. L. W. *Nature* **428**, 724–726 (2004).
3. Kaaret, P. *et al. Mon. Not. R. Astron. Soc.* **348**, 632–654 (2004).
4. Fabbiano, G., Zezas, A. & Murray, S. S. *Astrophys. J.* **554**, 1035–1043 (2001).
5. van der Marel, R. P. in *Coevolution of Black Holes and Galaxies* (ed. Ho, L. C.) (Cambridge Univ. Press, in the press).
6. Gurkan, M. A., Freitag, M. & Rasio, F. A. *Astrophys. J.* **604**, 632–654 (2004).
7. Bonnell, I. A. & Bate, M. R. *Mon. Not. R. Astron. Soc.* **336**, 659–669 (2002).
8. McCrady, N., Gilbert, A. M. & Graham, J. R. *Astrophys J.* **597**, 240–252 (2003).
9. Kaaret, P. *et al. Mon. Not. R. Astron. Soc.* **321**, L29–L31 (2001).
10. King, A. R., Davies, M. B., Ward, M. J., Fabbiano, G. & Elvis, M. *Astrophys. J.* **552**, L109–L112 (2001).
11. Begelman, M. C. *Astrophys. J.* **551**, 897–906 (2001).

Black

In "Hawking Slays His Own Paradox, but Colleagues Are Wary," Charles Seife explains that new work by the famous astrophysicist Steven Hawking questions how well a black hole's "food," or the matter it pulls in, gets "digested." The basic problem is that even though matter is lost forever in a black hole, the components of the matter may not be completely lost. Such information could be symbols formed by ink on paper, magnetic patterns on a computer disk, or the way the parts of any object fit together.

If bits of information are just crushed out of existence, then the total quantity of information in our universe must be steadily declining. Going against his previous theory that all matter and information is destroyed in a black hole, Hawking now has changed his mind. He had previously discovered a way for information to leak out of a black hole, thereby keeping the amount of information in the universe constant. The same amount of energy that went in also came out. So, just as black holes conserve matter and energy, they may also conserve information. In other words, information cannot be destroyed, just rearranged.

Hawking's new position, as this article explains, is that matter and energy are never really completely trapped in the black hole to begin with, thus eliminating any conflict with the basic law of conservation of energy. —RV

"Hawking Slays His Own Paradox, but Colleagues Are Wary"
by Charles Seife
Science, July 30, 2004

DUBLIN, IRELAND—In a public appearance that drew worldwide media coverage, Stephen Hawking claimed last week that he had solved one of the most important problems in physics: whether black holes destroy the information they swallow. Speaking at a conference here in a lecture hall packed with physicists and reporters, the University of Cambridge professor reversed his long-standing position and argued that information survives. As a result, Hawking conceded the most famous wager in physics and handed over an encyclopedia to the winner of the bet.

"It is great to solve a problem that has been troubling me for nearly 30 years," Hawking said during his presentation. Other physicists, however, doubt that Hawking has solved the long-lived puzzle. "It doesn't seem to me to be convincing," says John Friedman, a physicist at the University of Wisconsin, Milwaukee.

The question of what happens to information when it falls into a black hole goes to the heart of a central idea in modem physics. Just as scientists in the 19th century figured out that energy can be neither created nor destroyed, many 20th century physicists concluded that information is also conserved. If true, information conservation would be one of the most important principles in science—perhaps more profound even than conservation

of mass and energy. Unfortunately, there was a big obstacle: black holes.

When an object falls into a black hole, its mass and energy leave an observable imprint by making the black hole more massive. According to general relativity, however, any information the object carries is irretrievably lost: An outside observer couldn't tell whether the black hole had swallowed a ton of lead, a ton of feathers, or a ton of Ford Pintos. If black holes can destroy information in this way, information conservation cannot be a universal law.

The debate raged for decades whether black holes were an incurable exception to the permanence of information. In the 1970s, Hawking and some of his colleagues, including Kip Thorne of the California Institute of Technology (Caltech) in Pasadena, argued that black holes trump information. Others, such as Caltech's John Preskill, argued that some undiscovered loophole would keep information safe until the black hole somehow disgorged it. In 1997, Hawking and Thorne made a wager with Preskill; the winner was to receive an encyclopedia of his choice, from which information can always be retrieved.

At the Dublin conference, Hawking conceded the bet. Using a mathematical technique known as the Euclidean path integral method, Hawking proved to his own satisfaction that information is not, in fact, destroyed when it falls into a black hole. "If you jump into a black hole, your mass-energy will be returned to our universe . . . in a mangled form which contains the information about what you were like, but in a state where it cannot be easily recognized," said Hawking. That implies that black holes are not portals to other universes, a possibility Hawking himself had suggested. "I'm sorry to disappoint science-fiction fans," he said.

In conceding the bet, Hawking presented Preskill with *Total Baseball: The Ultimate Baseball Encyclopedia.* Thorne, however, refused to admit defeat. "I have chosen not to concede because I want to see more detail," he said, but added, "I think that Stephen is very likely right."

Others are less certain. Friedman, for one, has doubts about Hawking's mathematical method. Quantum field theorists are happy to use the Euclidean path integral technique for problems involving particles and fields, but most gravitational theorists avoid it because it produces equations riddled with hard-to-reconcile infinities. They prefer a more straightforward "Lorentzian" approach to gravity. Nobody has proven that the two methods always give the same results. "I'm skeptical whether the Euclidean path integral method generally represents the evolution of spacetime that is really Lorentzian," says Friedman. If not, then Hawking's conclusion may be an artifact of the mathematical method rather than a general result. Another reason for skepticism, Friedman says, is that Hawking's calculation takes a sum over all possible idealized black hole locations and all observers in the universe, but the results don't seem to apply to a specific black hole and a specific observer.

In part because of the Euclidean method, Hawking's work doesn't seem to yield any insight into how black holes preserve or release information—

whether all the pent-up information bursts forth at once, or whether it trickles out as subtle correlations in radiation coming from the black hole. Even Preskill says he wishes that Hawking's argument made more physical sense and could be expressed in more conventional mathematical terms. "If one could extract from the calculation an understanding that could be reproduced in a purely Lorentzian calculation, that would help a lot," he says.

Despite his doubts, Preskill has no qualms about accepting *Total Baseball*. "The terms were that the winner would receive the encyclopedia when the other party concedes," he says. "I don't have to agree."

Reprinted with permission from Seife, Charles, "Hawking Slays His Own Paradox, But Colleagues Are Wary," *Science* 305:586 (2004). © 2004 AAAS.

A neutron star is a collapsed star, which is extremely dense. There are certain types of neutron stars, though, that are called magnetars because they have magnetic fields a thousand times stronger than ordinary neutron stars. It is believed that, because they spin at such fast rates, an electrical dynamo inside the star is created, which produces an extremely intense magnetic field.

In time, however, these magnetic fields act to slow the neutron star's spin by robbing angular momentum from the star itself. This is a case in which the drag of the magnetic field represents a nonconserved force. The drag dissipates the energy of the neutron star's rotation. The angular momentum is conserved, however, because the rotational energy is transferred back into the magnetic field.

This conservation of energy sustains the extremely powerful magnetic field, which, in turn, keeps tapping momentum from the system. The following article explores this unique system in which the conservation of energy and momentum sustains the dynamic magnetar system. —RV

From "'Magnetar' Discovery Solves 19-Year-Old Mystery"
by Dave Dooling
NASA.gov, May 20, 1998

When you have eliminated all other possibilities, Sherlock Holmes instructed, whatever remains, however improbable, must be the answer.

In the mysterious case of the Soft Gamma Repeaters, or SGRs, the answer appears to be a magnetar, a neutron star with a super-strong magnetic field a thousand trillion times stronger than Earth's.

Indeed the magnetic field actually slows the star's rotation and causes starquakes that pump enough energy into the surrounding gases to generate bursts of soft gamma radiation. These led to discovery of the first SGR in 1979. For almost two decades, scientists speculated about the source, and eventually proposed a new class of highly magnetized stars—magnetars.

"The importance of this discovery goes beyond just adding a new oddity to the list of star types," said Dr. Chryssa Kouveliotou, the lead scientist on the discovery. "It ties together two rare, very peculiar classes of stars we have been puzzling over, and puts the evolution of neutron stars and even galaxies in a new light." It may also swell the population of our galaxy to include a few hundred million undiscovered magnetars . . .

Kouveliotou works for the Universities Space Research Association (USRA) at NASA's Marshall Space Flight Center. Working with her were Dr. Jan van Paradijs of the University of Amsterdam and the University of Alabama in Huntsville, Dr. Stefan Dieters of the University of Alabama in Huntsville, both working at NASA's Marshall Space Flight Center (MSFC) in Huntsville Ala., and Dr. Tod Strohmayer of NASA's Goddard Space Flight Center in Greenbelt, Md.

Looking for a Suspect

Their find strongly supports the magnetar theory offered in 1992 by astrophysicists Dr. Robert Duncan of the University of Texas at Austin and Dr. Christopher Thompson of the University of North Carolina at Chapel Hill. It's a dynamic model that has the neutron star going through a violent afterlife lasting about 10,000 years. Many colleagues discounted the concept, saying that internal pressures and other factors would keep a star from generating such an intense field.

"We were just trying to understand the origin of the magnetic fields of radio pulsars, which are the ordinary, familiar type of neutron stars," Duncan said.

Neutron stars are left when a massive star expends itself in a supernova. Most become pulsars when rotation of the neutron star's magnetic field produces a repeating, clocklike signal in radio, light, even X-rays and gamma rays. One mystery is why a large number of supernovas create magnificent nebulas yet leave no pulsar at the center. This anomaly poses a problem for theorists trying to calculate the rates of star births and deaths and, eventually, the ages of galaxies and the universe.

"The pulsar problem seemed rather subtle because the known pulsar magnetic fields, although enormous on terrestrial scales, are actually very weak compared to what is possible in forming neutron stars," Duncan continued. "It was much easier to find solutions with much stronger fields. Finally we began to wonder: Well, if much more strongly-magnetized stars did form, what would they look like? Only then did we make the connection with SGRs."

SGRs were not recognized as separate class until 1986 even though all three had been seen in 1979.

The Telltale Outburst

On March 5, 1979, gamma ray detectors on nine spacecraft across our solar system recorded an intense radiation spike. It was just 2/10th of a second long—with as much energy as the sun releases in 1,000 years—followed by a 200-second emission that showed a clear 8-second pulsation period (most SGR bursts release as much energy as the sun releases in one year). The position tied the burst to a supernova remnant known as N49 in the Large Magellanic Cloud.

Immediately, scientists recognized something odd. N49's youth—it's only a few thousand years old—contrasted with its 8-second spin, typical of a much older neutron star.

Something was putting the brakes on it.

The mystery expanded in 1986 when astrophysicists, meeting in Toulouse, France, realized that they had two more objects like this. Each emitted low-energy gamma rays. And each emitted repeated bursts (most gamma ray bursts are one-time events).

Thus, they were dubbed Soft Gamma Repeaters, or SGR. The object associated with N49 was designated SGR 0526-66 (the numbers indicate the position in the sky). The others are SGR 1806-20 at 14 kiloparsecs—one of the most active—and 1900+14, both in the Milky Way.

Theories abounded, but no one could be certain of the cause. So, it remained what Holmes would call "quite a three-pipe problem" until it became a three-satellite problem 10 years later.

In November 1996, the Burst and Transient Source Experiment aboard the Compton Gamma Ray Observatory detected SGR 1806-20 flaring up again. Kouveliotou used time she was allotted on Rossi X-ray Timing Explorer to take a closer look at the X-ray activities that followed.

During Nov. 5–18, 1996, RXTE captured several hours worth of data as bursts came in a "bunching" mode that had not been seen before. Following her observations, RXTE kept watching SGR 1806-20 to provide data for Strohmayer who was allotted time to observe during SGR 1806-20's quiescent phase. The result was a complementary data set that led to collaboration.

"Combining our data gave us both the capability to make a more sensitive search as well as provide a way to verify each others analysis of the data," said Strohmayer.

Reading the Evidence

As the name implies, RXTE carries instruments that read data quickly. Where most telescopes really take time exposures, RXTE Proportional Counter Array acts like a fast electronic counter which, combined with its size, was highly effective in searching for a pattern in the X-rays.

"I found a candidate periodic signal at 7.5 seconds in Chryssa's data, but we needed to have confirmation that the signal was also in Tod's dataset before we would be convinced it was real," remarked Dieters. The study was complicated by the need to carefully remove the data segments which had SGR bursts in them. "When you're looking for such a weak pulsar signal, the bursts could totally mask the modulations."

Then they looked through older data gathered by Japan's Advanced Satellite for Cosmology and Astrophysics (ASCA) in 1993. It had observed SGR 1806-20 while it was not bursting and was instrumental in establishing that the SGR was associated with a supernova remnant.

"When you know what period you are looking for it gives you a great advantage in sensitivity," remarked Strohmayer. "Finding the pulsed signal in the RXTE data allowed us to go back and also find it in the ASCA data, this removed the last shred of doubt that the pulsed signal could possibly be from another, previously unknown object in the RXTE field of view."

Between the ASCA and RXTE observations, SGR 1806-20 had slowed by 8/1,000th of a second. The difference would be miniscule except that it happened in less than four years to an object with more mass than our sun.

To test her finding, Kouveliotou asked Jeff Kommers of the Massachusetts Institute of Technology, another colleague, to check the data. Using a different approach, he came up with 7.5-seconds.

"That was the clincher," Kouveliotou said. "Two good data sets and two different methods of analysis gave the same answer."

Having established that SGR 1806-20 is associated with a pulsar and is slowing, rapidly, the team asked what might fit that profile.

In science, proving what something is often involves proving what it is not. Scientists suspected that SGRs are magnetars, but first they had to eliminate objects other than pulsars as the sources, and then eliminate possibilities other than magnetars as the answer.

The first possibility was simple accretion where material from another star is scooped up by the pulsar, or the magnetar.

Radio telescope observations by team member Dale Frail at the National Radio Astronomy Observatory helped rule out the accretion model. He showed that SGR 1806-20 coincides with a supernova remnant, SNR G10.0-0.3, whose radio broadcasts suggest a compact shape. It is also may be orbiting a nearby massive blue star every 10 years.

But 1806's own stellar wind is too powerful to let material fall inward, so it can't be an accreting pulsar.

Narrowing the Field

That leaves a single suspect.

"We found that the pulsar was slowing down at a rate that suggested a magnetic field strength of about 800 trillion Gauss, a field strength similar to that for so called magnetars predicted by previous theoretical work," said Kouveliotou.

By comparison, Earth's magnetic field is a mere 0.6 Gauss at the poles, and the best we can sustain in laboratories on the ground is 1 million Gauss—and that's in a small volume. Normal radio pulsars reach about 1 trillion to 5 trillion Gauss, strong but still short of a magnetar.

"If the field really is this strong," notes Kouveliotou, "then magnetism itself can keep the star hot—about 10 million degrees C (18 million deg. F) at the surface—and power the X-rays coming from its rotating surface."

"At the surface of the star a chunk of magnetizable metal like iron would feel a force equal to 150 million times the Earth's gravitational pull on it," added Strohmayer.

At this intensity, the magnetic field's movements wrinkle the crust of the neutron star and cause starquakes that are the source of the soft gamma-ray bursts.

Neutron stars are the only stars with a solid surface, a 1-km (0.6 mile) deep crust covering a thick fluid of neutrons over a superfluid—or possibly solid—core of subatomic particles.

"In ordinary neutron stars the crust is stable, but in magnetars, the crust is stressed by unbearable forces as the colossal magnetic field drifts through it," said Duncan. "This deforms the crust and sometimes cracks it." Violent seismic waves then shake the star's surface, generating Alfven waves—the electromagnetic equivalent of a Slinky toy—which energize clouds of particles above the surface of the star.

It also drags the star down, slowing it to about a 10-second period in just 10,000 years, about the age and speed of SGR 1806-20.

Eventually, the magnetars may become yet another oddity.

"We know six Anomalous X-ray Pulsars (AXPs) that are different from the bulk of the X-ray pulsars," said van Paradijs, who won the 1997 Rossi Prize for identifying the first optical counterpart for a gamma ray burst. "In terms of colors, the X-ray colors of the anomalous pulsars were very red compared to what you might call the blue normal pulsars." Their rotational periods also slow faster than other stars.

"Third, their pulse periods were close together," said van Paradijs. "All of them were like 6 to 10 seconds, which is very different from what you find with normal X-ray pulsars, which have pulse periods as short as less than a tenth of a second and as long as half an hour."

Since they slow down rapidly, then only a handful would be active for us to observe.

"So that even though there may be many of them, most of them are inactive, dead, so to say, lying in the graveyard," van Paradijs said. If the 10 or so SGRs and AXPs are magnetars, each less than 10,000 years old, then they probably form about once every thousand years.

"I think that conservatively 1 million magnetars have formed in our galaxy, and perhaps as many as 30 to 100 million," Duncan added.

Many of the supernova remnants that lack pulsars actually have them in the form of invisible, dead pulsars that exploded as supernovas, sputtered as SGRs concealing magnetars, then faded through the AXP stage to become invisible. Some may be made visible with more sensitive instruments like NASA/Marshall's Advanced X-ray Astrophysics Facility slated for launch in December 1997.

"Our plans are to go back to that source with RXTE, and hopefully with AXAF, and make more sensitive observations," Kouveliotou. "This is just starting. I'm looking forward to a hot debate on the subject."

Courtesy of NASA.

Web Sites

Due to the changing nature of Internet links, the Rosen Publishing Group, Inc., has developed an online list of Web sites related to the subject of this book. This site is updated regularly. Please use this link to access the list:

http://www.rosenlinks.com/cdfp/cwps

For Further Reading

Challoner, Jack, and Clive Streeter. *Eyewitness: Energy.*
New York, NY: DK Publishing, Inc., 2000.

Cooper, Christopher. *Forces and Motion: From Push to
Shove.* Chicago, IL: Heinemann Library, 2003.

Cunningham, James, and Norman Herr. *Hands-On
Physics Activities with Real-Life Applications: Easy-
to-Use Labs and Demonstrations for Grades 8–12.*
San Francisco, CA: Jossey-Bass, Inc., 2002.

Cutnell, John D., and Kenneth W. Johnson. *Physics.*
Hoboken, NJ: John Wiley & Sons, Inc., 2003.

Feynman, Richard, et al. *Six Easy Pieces: Essentials of
Physics Explained by Its Most Brilliant Teacher.*
New York, NY: Perseus Publishing, 1996.

Lafferty, Peter. *Eyewitness: Force and Motion.* New
York, NY: DK Publishing, Inc., 1999.

Bibliography

Barry, Patrick. "A Little Physics and a Lot of String." NASA.gov. July 9, 2000. Retrieved October 27, 2004 (http://science.nasa.gov/headlines/y2000/ast09jun_1.htm).

Bartusiak, Marcia. "Catch a Gravity Wave." *Astronomy*, October 2000.

Besenbacher, Flemming, and Jens K. Norskov. "How to Power a Nanomotor." *Science*, November 24, 2000.

Carusi, Andrea, Giovanni B. Valsecchi, Germano D'Abramo, and Andrea Boattini. "Deflecting NEOs in Route of Collision with the Earth." *Icarus*, March 7, 2002, p. 417.

Chown, Marcus. "Black Holes 'Detonating All Over Our Galaxy.'" *New Scientist*, November 28, 2001.

Clark, Rod, and Bob Wadsworth. "A New Spin on Nuclei." *Physics World*, July 1998.

Dooling, Dave. "'Magnetar' Discovery Solves 19-Year-Old Mystery." NASA.gov. May 20, 1998. Retrieved October 27, 2004 (http://science.msfc.nasa.gov/newhome/headlines/ast20may98_1.htm).

Haisch, Bernard, and Alfonso Rueda. "Prospects for an Interstellar Mission: Hard Technology Limits but Surprising Physics Possibilities." *Mercury*, July/August 2000.

Irion, Robert. "Crushed by Magnetism." *Science*, April 23, 2004, p. 534.

Jackson, Deborah J. "Solar Sail Technology Development." NASA.gov. March 22, 2002. Retrieved October 27, 2004 (http://solarsails.jpl.nasa.gov).

Jacob, M. "Fundamental Physics from Space and in Space." *Advances in Space Research*, December 2003, p. 1197.

Kokubo, Eiichiro, Shigeru Ida, and Junichiro Makino. "Evolution of a Circumterrestrial Disk and Formation of a Single Moon." *Icarus*, March 9, 2000, p. 419.

Lissauer, Jack J. "It's Not Easy to Make the Moon." *Nature*, September 25, 1997, p. 327.

McCrady, Nate. "The Missing Black Hole Link." *Nature*, April 15, 2004, p. 704.

McKee, Maggie. "Stray Star May Have Jolted Sedna." *New Scientist*, July 27, 2004.

NASA. "The Missing Moon of Sedna." NASA.gov. April 14, 2004. Retrieved October 27, 2004 (http://science.nasa.gov/headlines/y2004/14apr_sedna2.htm).

Overbye, Dennis. "Songs of the Galaxies, and What They Mean." *New York Times*, August 3, 2004.

Perkins, John. "Fusion Energy: The Agony, the Ecstasy and Alternatives." *Physics World*, November 1997.

Phillips, Tony. "Interplanetary Low Tide." NASA.gov. May 4, 2000. Retrieved October 27, 2004 (http://science.nasa.gov/headlines/y2000/ast04may_1m.htm).

Preuss, Paul. "Dark Energy Fills the Cosmos." *Berkeley Lab Research Review*, June 1, 1999.

Seife, Charles. "Gravity Probe to Give Einstein High-Precision Test." *Science*, April 16, 2004, p. 385.

Seife, Charles. "Hawking Slays His Own Paradox, but Colleagues Are Wary." *Science*, July 30, 2004, p. 586.

Watson, Andrew. "Accelerator Gets Set to Explore Cosmic Bias." *Science*, August 7, 1998, p. 764.

Index

Forman, William, 117, 118, 120
Forward, Robert, 28, 37, 145
Frail, Dale, 177
Frauendorf, Stefan, 47
Friedman, John, 168, 170
fuel, 16–17

G

galaxy growth, 121–122
gamma-ray bursts (GRBs),
    150–153, 160, 161, 175,
    178, 179
Gebhardt, Karl, 121
Gravity Probe B (GP-B)
    experiment, 131–132
    goals of, 128, 129–130, 131
    history of, 130
gravity waves, 139–140,
    141–142, 143, 146

H

Hawking, Stephen, 119
    black hole information
        theory, 167, 168, 169–170
    controversy, 170–171
Hawking radiation, 152
*Hazards Due to Comets and
    Asteroids*, 108
Hoyt, Robert, 25, 28
Hulse, Russell, 142

I

Ibrahim, Alaa, 160
Institute for High Energy
    Physics, 19
intermediate mass black
    holes, 162
    explanation of, 163–164
    mass segregation, 162–163
    super star clusters theory,
        164–165

and ultraluminous X-ray
    sources (ULXs), 164,
    165, 166

J

Jack, C., 38
Jet Propulsion Laboratory, 16
Jones, Christine, 118

K

Kaspi, Victoria, 159, 160
Kepler, Johannes, 31, 32
Kinney, Anne, 132
Koekemoer, Anton, 122,
    123, 124
Kommers, Jeff, 177
Kouveliotou, Chryssa, 155, 158,
    173, 176, 177, 178, 180
Kuiper Belt, 103, 104–105

L

laser beams, 12, 20–22
Laser Interferometer
    Gravitational-Wave
    Observatory (LIGO), 137,
    138, 140, 147, 149
    goals of, 139, 143, 148
    history of, 143–145
Lattimer, James, 157
Lazzarini, Albert, 147, 148
Lebo, George, 81
Levison, Hal, 105, 106
Loeb, Abraham, 118,
    121, 123
Lorentzian method, 170, 171
Lyutikov, Maxim, 161

M

magnetars
    explanation of, 155, 160,
        171, 174, 180

history of, 158, 172, 174–176
research of, 159–162
theory of, 173–174
Matthey, Christina, 151
Moon
characteristics of, 83, 84
"giant impact" formation scenario, 91–101
theories on origins of, 82, 83–86, 90–91, 101–102
Morbidelli, Alessandro, 105
Mottelson, Ben, 43

N

nanomotors
benefits of, 62, 63–64
constructing of, 64, 67
low-energy electron microscope (LEEM), 64–65, 66
scanning tunneling microscope (STM), 64, 66
nanotubes, 40
National Oceanic and Atmospheric Administration (NOAA), 31
near Earth objects (NEOs) deflection method
benefits of, 109
disadvantages of, 109–110, 111, 114
explanation of, 107, 108
study of, 110–114
neutron stars
characteristics of, 153, 154
and magnetism, 157
theories on, 155
Newton, Isaac
second law of motion, 29, 32
third law of motion, 11, 36, 107
N49, 174, 175
nuclear fission
disadvantages of, 54–55
safety of, 54–55
nuclear fusion
benefits of, 52–53
explanation of, 51
inertial fusion energy (IFE), 58–61
research of, 56, 61–62
safety of, 54–55
stellarator, 57, 58
tokamak approach, 53, 56, 57, 58, 59
nucleus
and angular momentum, 43, 44, 45, 47–48
rotation of, 41, 42–51

O

Oort cloud, 103, 104, 105
Ostriker, Jeremiah, 126
Otwinowski, Stanislaw, 151

P

Parkinson, Brad, 130
Perlmutter, Saul, 125, 126, 127
Preskill, John, 169, 170, 171

R

Rainwater, James, 43
Rees, Martin, 153
rockets and propulsion-mass problem, 12, 13–15
RXTE Proportional Counter Array, 176, 177

S

Sanders, Gary, 139
Saulson, Peter, 149
Schwarz, Andreas, 136

About the Editor

Ray Villard is news director for the Space Telescope Science Institute at Johns Hopkins University. He has received several NASA service awards for his contribution to the Hubble telescope project and has worked as an associate editor for *Astronomy* magazine and *Star & Sky* magazine. He also teaches astronomy courses and hosts public seminars through Johns Hopkins University, the Smithsonian Institution, and Howard Community College. Villard holds an MS in science communication from Boston University and is the author of *Large Telescopes: Inside and Out* and the forthcoming *Infinite World: An Illustrated Voyage to Planets Beyond Our Sun.*

Photo Credits

Front cover (clockwise from top right): "Infinite Textures" © Comstock Images Royalty-Free Division; "Swinging Clock Pendulum" © William James Warren/ Corbis; "Liquid Crystal" © Getty Images; background image of gyroscope © Getty Images; portrait, Isaac Newton © Library of Congress, Prints and Photographs Division. Back cover: top image "Electrons Orbiting Nucleus" © Royalty-Free/Corbis; bottom: "Liquid Crystal" © Getty Images.

Designer: Geri Fletcher; Series Editor: Nicholas Croce